T0165822

CHICAGO
HAUNTED HANDBOOK

AMERICA'S
HAUNTED ROAD TRIP

CHICAGO
HAUNTED HANDBOOK

**99 Ghostly Places You Can Visit
in and Around the Windy City**

jeff morris
vince sheilds

clerisy press

CHICAGO HAUNTED HANDBOOK
© 2013 by Jeff Morris and Vince Sheilds

ALL RIGHTS RESERVED. No portion of this book may be reproduced in any fashion, print, facsimile, or electronic, or by any method yet to be developed, without express permission of the copyright holder.

For further information, contact the publisher at:
Clerisy Press
306 Greenup Street
Covington, KY 41011
www.clerisypress.com
A division of Keen Communications

CATALOGING-IN-PUBLICATION DATA IS AVAILABLE FROM THE LIBRARY OF CONGRESS

ISBN 978-1-57860-527-9; eISBN 978-157860-528-6

Distributed by Publishers Group West
Printed in the United States of America
First edition, first printing

Cover design by Scott McGrew
Text design by Annie Long
Cover and interior photos provided by the authors unless otherwise noted.

CONTENTS

SECTION I cemeteries

SECTION II bars and restaurants

SECTION III roads and bridges

SECTION IV parks

SECTION V museums, theaters, hotels and other buildings

ACKNOWLEDGMENTS

WE WOULD LIKE TO START by thanking all of the behind-the-scenes people who made this book possible. During our countless hours of research into this vast array of haunted locations, we were helped by so many people who either wished to remain anonymous or whose names we never learned. It almost seems unfair that those who have helped us so tremendously not be individually mentioned in this section. For this reason, we feel that these particular folks should be acknowledged first. You have our most sincere apologies for not mentioning you by name, and you have our equally sincere gratitude for your insights.

Next, we would like to thank a few people and organizations who helped us with the daunting amount of research necessary to complete a book of this breadth. Without these dedicated individuals, this book would not have been possible. The Chicago Public Library and the Elgin Public Library provided not only assistance with our research, but also the necessary resources to complete it. Also, we thank David Scott from Ipra Illinois Para for making us aware of the fascinating stories behind the Manteno State Hospital when we ran into him at Scarefest.

Finally, we would like to extend individual thanks to our family, friends, and associates.

Vince: First and foremost, my old man and my grandfather, you helped with this book more than you could know. I can still hear Grandpa saying, "Walk softly, and carry a big stick."

Steven Fuller, Frank Rosko, and Tiffany Sawczenko: You all helped lay the foundation for, and I could not have asked for better pals with which to conduct, our paranormal investigations. I would also like to thank my friends Dylan Raye and Darleen Schillaci.

Tim McCauley: Out of all of my friends, I've known you the longest. And that probably gives you the most reasons not to be my friend anymore. It's this fact that makes me appreciate having you around even more.

Steve and Chris: You're my two favorite brothers. Thanks for being around.

Kelsey Tate: I'll never forget what you said to me one day. You said, "Vince, you're an idiot." But then, shortly after, you told me to not be afraid of being an individual."

I would like to think that I have taken your advice, so thanks.

Mom and Mike: Stay weird. I love you guys, and I never would have been involved with this book if it weren't for your guidance.

Jeff: I can't express my gratitude enough toward people like you who have encouraged and supported me throughout the creation of this book.

Amy, Koen, and Koda: As my family, you have allowed me the necessary time to both work on the book at home and travel to Chicago for research. It's essential to also note that my parents have been very generous and supportive during the writing of this book, and they also deserve my most sincere thanks.

Garett Merk: The coauthor of two of my previous books, you drove me to Chicago to visit many of the places that would eventually end up in this book. Thank you. Ryan Vehr also tagged along and was gracious enough to take the floor while Garett and I slept on the couch and chair.

Archer Woods Cemetery (Mount Glenwood Memory Gardens West), see page 5

FOREWORD

IMAGINE.

IMAGINE YOU HAD THE ABILITY to go to any place in the world at any time in history. To walk the streets of Jerusalem in Biblical times. To sit in the stands at the Roman Coliseum while gladiators dueled below. To watch any great battle of history from the sidelines. To experience any great disaster or event and to see it as it really happened.

Where would you go? When would it be?

If I had the ability to transport myself to any place at any time in history, I would go to Chicago in 1893. This was the year of the World's Fair—probably the greatest World's Fair in history—which occurred in Chicago in what is today Jackson Park, on the shores of Lake Michigan.

They called it the White City. The buildings, temporary, were meant to survive for only the duration of the event, and all were painted white. At night, electricity lit the fairgrounds. At the time, onlookers described it as magical. Few of these folks had electricity themselves. Some had never seen electric lights illuminate a building. The fairgrounds appeared as bright as if it were daytime. The future had arrived in Chicago; the warm glow of the lights symbolized brighter times to come, as a new age arrived in one fantastic event.

Incredible sights that would become staples of the approaching decades were first exhibited at the fair. The first Ferris wheel towered over the Midway. The first functioning zipper was showcased at this fair. So was Juicy Fruit gum, Pabst Blue Ribbon beer, and Cream of Wheat. During this extravaganza, a newspaper writer coined the term "Windy City" to describe Chicago, a name by which it is still known today. At the same time, pillars of the past were represented at the fair—most notably Buffalo Bill's Wild West Show.

Perhaps the most exciting battle taking place at the fair was that between Thomas Edison and Nikola Tesla. Edison championed his direct current technology, while Tesla promoted his safer, alternating-current technology, which, due to a win in a bidding war, ended up powering the lights at the fair. Still, Edison and Tesla maintained their own exhibits at the fair, where they demonstrated their individual electric technologies as the awed masses watched in wonder.

If I were transported to this place, I would feel as if I were standing at the threshold of the future. Its people didn't know it yet, but the world was about to change. At last, our planet was coming of age. Technology would begin to increase exponentially.

People who lived in the world before the fair wouldn't have been able to fathom the world we live in today. Sure, they could anticipate what the future might bring, but they couldn't predict such boundless change. Imagine walking among those very buildings that contained the technology that would build our world. Imagine watching the people who were tasting the foods that would become the staples of our modern diet, or seeing the technology that would one day govern our lives. As you can tell, history fascinates me. And I can't imagine a more fascinating moment in history than Chicago in 1893.

This book presents a similar portal into the past. Upon reading this book, you will have the opportunity to delve into, and even experience, the past in a manner similar to traveling back in time. No one is sure what a ghost is, not even those who have seen and experienced them firsthand. Some argue that a ghost is just a form of energy that is left behind when a traumatic or important event occurs. Others say that a ghost is a person in a different form, living on after his or her mortal body has passed.

Whatever ghosts actually are, people tend to agree on one point about them: Ghosts tell stories about the past. This book collects the ghost stories of 100 different locations in the Chicagoland area. Events that have built not only the city of Chicago, but America as a whole, have happened numerous times throughout this city's history. Great disasters, such as the wreck of the *SS Eastland* and the crash of American Airlines Flight 191, have occurred here. The ghosts that were left behind tell rich and captivating stories. Sometimes, when you are present at one of these sites, it can feel as though you are actually experiencing that very moment in history.

Is our fascination with ghosts a fascination with what happens to us after death, or is it simply a fascination with the past? Are ghosts nature's way of preserving history? Are ghosts telling firsthand accounts of events that the public is beginning to forget? Are ghosts the present's reminder of the past? These same questions, and many more, may spring to your mind as you are reading this book.

Often, when ghosts are telling the story, the event that occurred at the location they haunt is a sad one. Ghosts may be trying to remind us of past tragedies. They may be hoping to ensure that those who perished will not be forgotten. And just maybe, they are trying to prevent the mistakes of the past from being repeated.

When I first started working on this book, I drove up to Chicago to visit many of the haunted locations that Vince and I planned to write about. During this first trip, I did not have time to visit each and every location, but I made sure that we stopped at Jackson Park. I wanted to stand on the very ground where the 1893 World's Fair took place.

It was after dark when we arrived. The park does not close until 11 p.m., so I had the opportunity to walk the grounds late at night. The site was completely empty and our car was the only one in the lot. Vince took some pictures and made some audio recordings on the Clarence Darrow Memorial Bridge while I walked on alone into the park.

I stood there in the black of night. Dim light poles lit the narrow walkways that crisscrossed the park. I faced the Museum of Science and Industry, the only surviving building from the fair, and imagined that I was at the fair itself. I imagined the people walking past me. I imagined the electricity building and the bright lights of the White City shining all around me.

I was a visitor from another time. Perhaps, in a way, I was invading their space. I entered their fairgrounds knowing what the world was becoming and not allowing them the adventure of discovering this new world for themselves.

I jumped as I clearly heard a voice behind me say, "Get out."

I turned.

There was no one there.

Happy ghosting!

—*Jeff Morris*

INTRODUCTION

CHICAGO: It's one of the brightest, most inviting places in the world. At the same time, it's one of the darkest, coldest places you'll ever find yourself. And yet, it's one of the warmest places on Earth—filled with hard-working people that would give you the shirts off their backs, even if you didn't ask.

Having lived in this city my whole life, I realize it has issues, but still there is a kind of inexplicable magnetism that keeps pulling me back. It's almost as if the city's deepest secrets—held within its cemeteries, deep within its willow and oak trees, and atop the towering John Hancock Center—are calling me to explore them. Sometimes, it almost feels like the very veins of this city are not necessarily its roads, people, or buildings, but the stories that live on and are begging to be heard and retold.

Although the formula of this handbook may seem simple, let me assure you, gathering the contents for the book was no easy task. Chances are, if you're currently reading this, you have probably picked up another haunted Chicago type of publication. To be honest, I have read them all. And the truth is, they are all pretty informative and do a decent job of telling stories about some of Chicago's most haunted locations.

Knowing this, we've tried to do something different with our *Chicago Haunted Handbook*. This time, we've only included locations that, one, we actually thought were haunted and, two, you can physically visit and investigate. This is the reason for omitting a place like Harpo Studios, which is impossible to visit unless you are Oprah herself or at least a worthy doppelganger. That said, we've still included favorites, such as Bachelor's Grove and Willowbrook Ballroom, but we've also added new places that you have probably never heard of, such as the Grease Factory, located in the small town of Huntley, or the California Clipper in Chicago's Humboldt Park neighborhood. There is no other book that includes information such as visiting hours, exact directions, history, and the ghost story for each of these locations.

I've learned so much about Chicago and Chicagoland in the past few years while collecting the information for this book, yet there is so much more out there for you to find for yourself. Hopefully, this handbook can guide you in the right direction.

Chicago is much more than a place to live; every nook and cranny has its own dark story to tell.

—*Vince Sheilds*

SECTION I

cemeteries

ALGONQUIN CEMETERY

Cary Road and Route 31, Algonquin, Illinois 60102

directions

From the center of Chicago, take I-90 West for about 26.5 miles to the Roselle Road exit. Keep right on the ramp toward Palatine/Little City and merge onto North Roselle Road. After about 1 mile, turn left onto West Algonquin Road and follow it for about 13 miles. Turn right onto Main Street. After about 0.5 mile, turn right onto Cary Road. The cemetery is on both sides of Cary Road.

history

The first settler in the Algonquin area was a man named Samuel Gillilan, who built a log cabin on the site of the cemetery. Eventually, Gillilan passed away, and the site on both sides of Cary Road was used as the cemetery for the village of Algonquin.

There is a story about a man who lived in the area who raped a woman. The man died soon thereafter and was buried at Algonquin Cemetery. Many felt that his burial in the cemetery was too good an end for a rapist and wanted something worse for him. A priestess who lived in the area visited the cemetery and drew a circle around the rapist's gravesite. She then cast a spell on the gravesite, forever binding the rapist to this spot.

ghost story

There are essentially two areas to find ghosts at this cemetery, but the section that borders Main Street, on the north side of Cary Road, houses the more pleasant ghosts. People have seen figures in this section of the cemetery and will often see orbs of light floating through the area at night. Voices are also heard in this part of the cemetery when there is no physical body present.

The other side of the cemetery, on the south side of Cary Road, has a much darker presence. The ghost of the rapist haunts this section of the cemetery but cannot leave the circle that was drawn by the priestess around his gravesite. If you stand on the gravesite of the rapist, you will apparently feel extreme discomfort. People who stand on the gravesite will report seeing figures running back and forth in the adjacent woods. Sometimes the ghost of a small boy will stand at the edge of the forest and watch anyone who stands on the rapist's grave. Other visitors to the cemetery will see the apparition of a man in a black suit standing on the site of the rapist's grave, watching any passersby menacingly. Angry whispers are heard in the area, and some people report being pushed by some unseen force or grabbed by the ankles when standing on or near the gravesite.

visiting

The cemetery is open from dawn until dusk, so it is closed at night. Your best bet for experiencing the ghost of the rapist is to go into the cemetery just before it closes at sunset. Many of the ghost legends surrounding this site occur at night, but you should not enter the cemetery after it closes or you will be subject to arrest for trespassing. The grave of the rapist is reportedly the one closest to the woods on the south side of the road that loops through the dark side of the cemetery. Some say that you can still see the vague imprint of a circle in the ground surrounding the gravesite.

The balls of light on the north side of the cemetery can be seen from Cary Road, which is, of course, open to the public throughout the night.

ARCHER WOODS CEMETERY
(Mount Glenwood Memory Gardens West)

8301 Kean Avenue, Willow Springs, Illinois 60480

directions

From the center of Chicago, travel south on I-55 for 13.5 miles to the exit for US 12 East and South La Grange Road. Follow South La Grange Road for about 3 miles and then turn left onto W 87th Street. Take a left onto South Kean Avenue. The cemetery will be on your right after about 0.5 mile.

history

Not much is known about the history of the ghost that haunts this cemetery. The cemetery itself was established in 1920 and has been accepting burials since that time, so the ghost could belong to any one of the thousands of people who were buried here.

There are many old and interesting headstones and monuments within the cemetery. Perhaps the most interesting of these monuments is called the Garden of Hymns monument, a stone wall topped with organ pipes.

ghost story

This area is a notoriously haunted part of Chicago. It is near the haunted Archer Avenue, Willowbrook Ballroom, Resurrection Cemetery, the haunted intersection of Kean and 95th Street, and St. James Sag Cemetery. Several ghost stories circulate about this cemetery. The most famous ghost of Archer Woods Cemetery is a woman in white who sobs just inside the front gate. The woman is most often seen by passing motorists after the cemetery has closed at sunset. These motorists report seeing a woman just inside the gates hunched over and crying. When they go up to her to see what is wrong, she vanishes into thin air.

This woman is also seen during the day. When witnesses encounter her during the day, they report entering the cemetery without seeing the woman. As they are leaving, though, witnesses find her hunched by the entrance, sobbing. Those who see her during the day will only see her on their way out, and never encounter her on their way into the cemetery.

Remarkably, there are many people who claim to have photographed the woman. Most often, these photographers will not realize that they have photographed the apparition until they get home and examine their photographs.

Beyond the sobbing woman, this cemetery boasts a handful of other strange happenings. People will sometimes get lightheaded and dizzy in the cemetery for no apparent reason. Others will hear the Garden of Hymns playing organ music. Still more will watch a black, horse-drawn hearse slow down in front of the cemetery, then vanish.

visiting

The cemetery is open from sunrise until sunset. Even though the gates are often left open throughout the night, it is illegal to enter the cemetery after nightfall. No matter; most all of the photographs of the sobbing woman have been taken during the day. Passing motorists who see the sobbing woman at night need not enter the cemetery, as they will see the woman sobbing behind the gates.

BACHELOR'S GROVE CEMETERY

5900 Midlothian Turnpike, Midlothian, Illinois 60445

directions

Bachelor's Grove Cemetery is rather difficult to find. From the center of Chicago, take I-94 East to I-57 South. Follow I-57 South for about 5 miles to Exit 353, the Burr Oak Avenue exit. Take your first right onto 127th Street and follow that for about 3 miles. Turn left onto South Pulaski Road and follow that for another 1.5 miles. Turn right onto Midlothian Turnpike. About 2.5 miles down the road, you will see a parking area on your right for the Rubio Forest Preserve. Park there. Cross Midlothian Turnpike, heading toward cell towers by the woods. To the right of the cell towers is a small path that runs into the woods. Follow that path for about a 0.25 mile into the woods, and you will come to the decrepit cemetery.

history

Until the 1960s, instead of angling at 143rd Street, Midlothian Turnpike continued straight, all the way to Ridgeland Avenue. But in the 1960s, the road was shut down at 143rd Street to vehicular traffic, leaving only a trail leading out into the woods. This stretch of road between the angling of Midlothian Turnpike and Bachelor's Grove Cemetery has a rather turbulent history for an area so remote.

Perhaps the most famous recorded death in the area occurred in the 1870s. A farmer was plowing a field across 143rd Street when something startled his horse. The horse ran across 143rd Street towards where the small pond exists today near the cemetery. As the farmer struggled to control his horse, he became entangled in the reins. When the horse arrived at the pond, and the plow began to sink into the water, the farmer was still hopelessly entangled. Unable to escape, he was slowly pulled under the water and drowned. This same pond would become a dumping ground for bodies of the victims of the gang wars of the 1920s.

This story is just a drop in the bucket of all of the troubling occurrences that have happened here since 1833, when four unmarried bachelors founded the settlement for which the cemetery is named. Many of the worst occurred in the 1960s and 1970s, after the road was shut down. Even before the road was closed, the area was a popular "lover's lane," where local teenagers hung around late into the night. Newly closed to access, the remote burial site was exposed to vandals, who destroyed what they could of the cemetery by tearing up or spray-painting its headstones. These headstones would be strewn about and discovered miles away. Local police would not even return the found headstones to the cemetery, knowing that they would just be taken again.

The 1960s and 1970s also saw Bachelor's Grove become a center for Satanic rituals. People would find dead animals strewn around the area, apparently victims of some dark sacrifice. Eventually, the vandalism and rituals all but stopped. Some thank the increased patrols of local law enforcement. Others say that something darker inside of those woods scared the vandals away.

ghost story

Some say that this cemetery is the most haunted place on Earth. People will experience the ghosts from the beginning of the trail off the Midlothian Turnpike all the way back to the cemetery and the pond just past it. Perhaps the most frequently seen ghosts here take the form of balls of light. These balls of light appear as either red or blue orbs that float down the path or through the woods directly adjacent to the path. Other witnesses only report feelings of discomfort while walking the path; they experience intangible feelings of dread or depression, or feel as though they are being watched by some unseen entity as they walk the trail.

Beyond these common ghost stories, a few highly unusual sightings have been reported in the area. One night, forest officials from the Rubio Forest Preserve were patrolling the area near the pond. Out of nowhere, they saw a horse pulling a plow run across the path toward the pond and then vanish without a trace. Others have seen a phantom house appear and disappear in the woods. The house has been seen on several occasions by people who had never heard the story of the phantom house before. Many of the accounts of this house are eerily similar. It is always a white, two-story farmhouse. There is a swing on the porch and a welcoming light burning in one of the downstairs windows. Legend has it that if you enter the house, you will be trapped there forever. Some stories report that as you approach the house, it seems to get farther and farther away, until it eventually vanishes into the distance.

As if these stories weren't enough to give this place its haunted reputation, there are numerous other tales told about the area. Most of these involve apparitions who walk the trail and cemetery and vanish without a trace. Some of these apparitions are men wearing brown robes and hoods. The most famous apparition, though, is that of a woman. She has been called "the white lady," "Mrs. Rodgers," and, most famously, "the Madonna of Bachelor's Grove." She has been photographed at least twice by people who did not see her when they took the photograph. She has been seen countless other times on the path or in the cemetery itself.

visiting

When visiting this place, the most important thing to keep in mind is to follow all of the local laws. This means that when you park, park your car at the Rubio Forest Preserve and not in the nearby driveways or along the road. Furthermore and most importantly, the path and cemetery close at sunset. You must not enter this area under any circumstances after the sun has set. Due to the turbulent history of the area, it is patrolled regularly, and you will be arrested if you attempt to visit at night.

BLUFF CITY CEMETERY

945 Bluff City Boulevard, Elgin, Illinois 60120

directions

From the center of Chicago, take I-290 West for 24.5 miles to Exit 5, the Thorndale Avenue exit. Turn left onto Thorndale Avenue. The road will change its name to Elgin O'Hare Expressway West, but stay straight for about 6.5 miles to the Lake Street exit. Turn right onto Lake Street and follow it for another 5.5 miles until angling left onto Bluff City Boulevard. Follow the road for 1 mile until you see the cemetery on your left.

history

The dead have been brought to these hallowed grounds since the cemetery came into existence in 1889. The cemetery is quite large, encompassing 108 acres of burial plots. The cemetery is bordered by gardens and imbues visitors with a sense of serenity as they enter. Although the name suggests that the cemetery is composed of hills and cliffsides, it is not. The name of the cemetery actually refers to a nickname for the surrounding town of Elgin and the bluffs that overlook the Fox River.

Perhaps the most convincing reason that ghosts have taken up residence in this particular cemetery involves another burial spot called Channing Cemetery (see Channing Park and School chapter). When Bluff City Cemetery was built in the late

1800s, the plan was to move the bodies from the old Channing Cemetery over to Bluff City. The problem was that Channing Cemetery was already so old that many of the headstones had been lost and many burials from the local mental asylum were made without headstones at all. Many of these bodies were inadvertently left at Channing, and when they were discovered, they were moved to Bluff City Cemetery without ceremony and without proper respect or care.

ghost story

The most commonly reported ghostly activity at the cemetery is little more than a feeling that visitors often experience upon entering the cemetery grounds. Visitors are said to get a very strong and distinctive feeling that they are being watched. This feeling is rarely ominous or scary, but is more often calming and peaceful. It is almost as if the spirits of loved ones who have passed are watching the mourners and somehow letting them know that everything will be all right.

While this feeling is the most common experience within the cemetery, people have captured evidence of other strange phenomena within the cemetery gates. Paranormal researchers have captured orbs, strange lights, and shadowy figures on camera while in the cemetery. When these strange photographic artifacts are examined, no earthly reason is discovered why they should be there.

visiting

The cemetery is open 7 a.m.–7:30 p.m. April–October; November–March, it is open 7 a.m.–4 p.m. You cannot access the cemetery outside of these posted hours. Many of the orbs and figures are seen and photographed during daylight hours. Much of the cemetery is visible from the adjacent public road, though, so you can still look into the cemetery at night in an attempt to see the mysterious lights that supposedly inhabit the grounds.

BURR OAK CEMETERY

4400 West 127th Street, Aslip, Illinois 60803

directions

From the center of Chicago, take I-94 East for about 6.5 miles to Exit 63, I-57 toward Memphis. Follow I-57 for another 5 miles to Exit 353 toward 127th Street. Take your first right onto 127th Street and follow it for another 3.5 miles. The cemetery will be on your right.

history

The history of this cemetery has been rocky from the beginning. The cemetery was created for the quickly growing African American population in Chicago during the early 20th century. After securing the land, a body was found in the local morgue that could be used to dedicate the cemetery. As the body was carried to the cemetery grounds to officially dedicate the cemetery, however, it was met with significant backlash. The predominantly white village of Aslip did not want a black cemetery anywhere near town. With the help of armed policemen, they turned the burial party around. Those determined to create an African American cemetery were not deterred. They enlisted the help of the sheriff's department and buried the body anyway.

The cemetery ran into additional issues a little further along in its history. It faced financial trouble and defaulted during The Great Depression, but it was ultimately saved. Like any cemetery, Burr Oak experienced some issues with vandalism during the middle part of the century, but it is the cemetery's recent history that has kept it in the news and perhaps instigated paranormal activity on its grounds.

In 2009, the Cook County Sheriff accused the owners of the cemetery of criminally mistreating the bodies at the cemetery. According to many accusations, countless corpses were dug up and thrown into mass graves in order to make room for more bodies. In other instances, headstones were allegedly removed and new burials were made on top of old burials. At capacity, the cemetery is able to hold 130,000 bodies. Currently, cemetery records indicate that there could be as many as 147,568 people buried here.

ghost story

During an investigation of illegal activity, it was discovered that one section of the cemetery experienced the most foul play. Thus, it was designated by the sheriff's office as "Crime Scene A." Most of the paranormal activity occurs in the area known as "Crime Scene A." People feel uncomfortable in this area. They feel like they are being watched or experience other indescribable sensations.

There are often reports of people walking through the cemetery at night. Whenever these figures are investigated, no one is ever found. Some suggest that the figures who aimlessly roam the cemetery at night are those whose bodies were moved during the grave desecration scandal and who are looking for their original graves.

visiting

The cemetery is open every day of the week except Sunday. It is open 8 a.m.–4 p.m. daily. During these hours, you may roam the cemetery in an attempt to experience some of the paranormal feelings that are often reported. Because the cemetery closes at 4 p.m., you will be unable to enter the cemetery at night to look for the roaming figures. However, there are public roads encircling the cemetery that remain open throughout the night. You can drive along these roads at night and peer into the cemetery in an attempt to see the lost figures roaming aimlessly around.

CALVARY CEMETERY

301 Chicago Avenue, Evanston, Illinois 60202

directions

From the center of Chicago, take North Lake Shore Drive for about 6 miles, then turn right onto Sheridan Road. Follow Sheridan Road for a little more than 2.5 miles. Sheridan continues through a narrow stretch between Lake Michigan and Calvary Cemetery.

history

There are many historical figures from the Chicagoland area buried in this cemetery. White Sox founder and ballpark namesake Charles Comiskey is buried here, as well as a mayor and prominent businessmen from the area. Those who are buried at the cemetery have little, if anything, to do with the ghost who haunts the place.

There are a couple of different historical accounts that may explain the strange ghost that is seen here. The first account describes an aviator at the nearby naval base who was doing maneuvers over Lake Michigan during World War II. While flying, the plane experienced a mechanical failure and crashed into Lake Michigan. Eventually, wreckage from the plane washed ashore near Calvary Cemetery, but the body of the aviator was never recovered. The second account is more verifiable than the first. On May 4, 1951, a flight instructor at the nearby Naval Air Station Glenview was flying out over Lake Michigan on a calm day. Up until this point, all other flights from the base were uneventful. After the flight instructor lost radio contact with the base, search parties were sent to look for him, but no traces were found. Two days later, his body washed up on the North Shore of Lake Michigan across Sheridan from Calvary Cemetery.

ghost story

The ghost here near Calvary Cemetery is one of the most frequently sighted apparitions in all of Chicagoland. People who drive down Sheridan around midnight will sometimes see this apparition walking across the road between Lake Michigan and the cemetery. The apparition takes the form of a man in his late 20s or early 30s who is covered with seaweed. There will be a slight green glow coming from him as he drags himself across the street towards the cemetery. After he crosses the street, he vanishes into the cemetery.

The locals are well aware of the ghost who crosses the street into the cemetery. They have even given him a name, "Seaweed Charlie."

visiting

This is one of Chicago's easiest ghosts to go looking for for a couple of reasons. First, the ghost is not in the cemetery, which closes before dark every night. The ghost crosses Sheridan Road just outside the cemetery gates, and the road is open throughout the night. The ghost is most often seen by passing motorists, who are able to drive up and down Sheridan Road in this area all night without fear of legal ramifications. Second, this ghost appears often. There are literally hundreds of reports of people who have seen this ghost. Sometimes, the ghost has even been reported to have disrupted traffic in the area. Witnesses will see cars ahead of them swerving to avoid hitting something, which they soon discover is a green glowing man covered with seaweed.

COUNTY FARM CEMETERY (Joliet Potter's Field)

880 Mission Boulevard, Joliet, Illinois 60431

directions

From the center of Chicago, take I-55 South for 40 miles to Exit 253 toward Joliet. Turn left onto US-52 East and follow this road for 2 miles. Turn right onto Infantry Drive and then, after 0.5 mile, right again onto County Farm Road. Take a left onto Mission Boulevard. You will need to park by the soccer fields. Standing on Mission Boulevard facing the field, you proceed to your right until you come upon a thin line of trees adjacent to a residential area, then follow that line of trees away from Mission Boulevard until you hit another small grove of trees. The cemetery is inside this grove.

history

The cemetery was founded in 1850 and belonged to Will County Farm. Will County Farm was a home for the elderly and the homeless. It is likely that many of these people were buried in the cemetery. Other poor people who could not afford a plot in another cemetery were also buried here over the years. Historians think that there could be as many as 150 people buried in the cemetery.

Throughout the cemetery, there are 48 stones. Most of the stones are marked with numbers instead of names, which suggests that multiple people are buried in each of the areas marked by the stones. Only one stone currently bears a name in the cemetery. It says "George Miller." He died in 1907.

In more recent years, the cemetery had fallen into complete disrepair. Broken headstones littered the ground. Bones from the deceased had surfaced and been taken by local wildlife. Local volunteers are working to fix up the cemetery, but its disrepair still echoes through the ghosts that haunt this potter's field.

ghost story

The cemetery itself has an air of sadness and despair. People who enter it are sometimes overwhelmed by this feeling. As soon as they step out of the cemetery, they are no longer sad. It is almost as if the cemetery has its own atmosphere of depression that only affects people when they are within the cemetery grounds.

Inside the cemetery, trees and bushes often rustle and move by themselves on windless days. When investigated, no cause for the rustling can be determined. Other witnesses have reported seeing glowing orbs of light floating through the cemetery.

Perhaps the strangest thing to happen here is that many photographs of the cemetery are distorted. Many photographers state that on certain days it is impossible to get a clear picture of the cemetery. Certain elements are out of focus for no reason. Other parts seem stretched beyond recognition.

visiting

The cemetery is open from sunrise until sunset. This is not optimal for ghost hunting here, but there are still some things that visitors are able to experience. The distorted photographs can be taken during daylight hours. The oppressive feelings of despair are experienced during both day and night. Unfortunately, the glowing orbs of light are only seen at night and the cemetery is too far from any adjacent roads to see after darkness falls.

EVANGELICAL CHURCH CEMETERY

3724 Washington Street, Oak Brook, Illinois 60523

directions

From the center of Chicago, take I-290 West for a little more than 13.5 miles to Exit 15A, I-294 South. Follow I-294 South for a little more than 3.5 miles and take the US-34 West exit. Turn right onto Ogden Avenue and then turn right onto North York Road after a little less than 0.5 mile. Take your second left onto Spring Road and then your first left onto Washington Street. The Faith Fellowship Church will be on your right. The cemetery is just to the west of the church, on the other side of the church from the road.

history

In 1852, a water-powered gristmill called the Graue Mill was constructed in Oak Brook. While on the outside the mill seemed unassuming, the building was actually used for secret but noble causes. This building was an important stop in the Underground Railroad, and countless escaped slaves would stop here before heading to Canada.

Unfortunately, many of these slaves did not make it to their final destinations. Some were caught and killed. Others succumbed to the brutal Chicago winter. Others simply committed suicide. While many used the mill as an important stepping stone to freedom, many more had experienced too much hardship by this point and could not make it farther. Many of the fleeing slaves who died in the area were buried in what is today the Evangelical Church Cemetery.

The cemetery became official in 1877, as burials were first officially recorded here. The Faith Fellowship Church next door was built in 1881. Today, the Graue Mill is a museum.

ghost story

Although not the best-known haunted place in the Chicagoland area, this cemetery is considered by those who know it to be one of the most haunted in not only the city, but the entire country. The cemetery is haunted by the ghosts of slaves who died in the area and were buried here.

Often, people who photograph the cemetery capture strange balls of light or inexplicable fogs in their photographs. People who enter feel an intangible energy within the cemetery grounds. They report that the atmosphere within the cemetery simply feels different from the atmosphere outside of the cemetery. Some people feel uncomfortable. Others feel like they are being watched or feel overcome with despair and hopelessness.

Apparitions are often seen in the cemetery. These apparitions take the form of escaped slaves. People commonly see emaciated and frightened African Americans within the cemetery who simply disappear, leaving witnesses wondering if they had even seen the figures in the first place.

visiting

Although there are no hours posted at the cemetery, the staff at the Faith Fellowship Church advise that the cemetery is only open from sunrise until sunset. The cemetery is not visible from the street after dark, so you will have to approach the cemetery during daylight hours. However, the apparitions in the cemetery are not often seen in the bright daylight hours. Your best chance of seeing them without trespassing is to go to the cemetery right at sunrise or sunset, or during a dreary, rainy day.

GRACELAND CEMETERY
4001 North Clark Street, Chicago, Illinois 60613

directions
From the center of Chicago, take US-41 North for about 4 miles to the Irving Park Road exit. Turn left onto Irving Park Road and follow it for about 1 mile. Turn right onto North Clark Street. The entrance to Graceland Cemetery will be on your right, at the corner.

history
From its inception in 1860, the cemetery has always been a private one. Its creator, Thomas Bryan, wanted it to stand apart from many local cemeteries of the time in

order to gain business. He wanted it to look like the most beautiful and peaceful place in the city. He hired landscape architects to design the grounds. Famous area sculptors created many of the tombstones. Bryan succeeded in making Graceland one of the most attractive spaces in the city.

Throughout the many years that the cemetery has been in operation, many of the area's most famous people have been buried here. The first white settler of Chicago, John Kinzie, is buried here. Assassinated Chicago mayor Carter Harrison is buried here. Department store magnate Marshall Field, private eye Allan Pinkerton, and Charles Dickens's brother are all also buried here.

One of the most famous markers at the cemetery is for a girl named Inez Clarke. Many verifiable historic documents regarding this girl have been lost to history. In fact, cemetery records state that no one named Inez Clarke is buried at the cemetery. Inez is more likely a girl named Inez Briggs, daughter of Mary Clarke from a previous marriage. According to many local legends, though, Inez Clarke (1873-1880 on her marker) was at a family picnic when she was struck by lightning and killed. Distraught, her family had a likeness of her built and placed in a glass box aboveground to mark where she was buried.

ghost story

Throughout the cemetery, people sometimes detect unexplainable drops in temperature. Perhaps this is caused by one of the departed residents walking past. These temperature fluctuations would be the most widespread hauntings in the cemetery, if not for two eerie monuments.

The first is called Eternal Silence, and it is the family stone for the Graves family. The marker is an admittedly creepy statue of a robed figure with a hood. Legend says that if you look into the face of the statue, you will catch a glimpse of your own death. Further, it is said that the statue is impossible to clearly photograph and that cameras will malfunction when aimed at the statue. Plenty of photographs exist of the statue, so apparently cameras do not malfunction all the time, but people do still report malfunctioning cameras from time to time when they attempt to photograph the statue.

The second monument is the statue of Inez Clarke. Strange sounds are often heard near the marker. People hear footsteps and whispers in this vicinity. They also hear crying. However, many of the more famous stories about the marker involve the statue itself. There are several accounts of the statue completely vanishing without a trace. A girl who resembles the statue has been seen wandering through the cemetery and then vanishing. This happens most often during thunderstorms, perhaps in reference to the supposed cause of the girl's death by lightning strike. Sometimes, people see the glass box, but it is completely empty. A particularly famous story of this phenomenon occurred in the late 1800s, when the night watchman at the cemetery experienced exactly that and fled the cemetery, never to return.

visiting

The cemetery is open daily, 8 a.m.–4:30 p.m. You may not enter the cemetery at any other times. Your best bets for experiencing something paranormal here would be to go to one of the two haunted monuments in the cemetery. You should try to take pictures of Eternal Silence to see if anything strange occurs and maybe approach the Inez Clarke marker during a thunderstorm.

HOLY SEPULCHER CEMETERY

6001 West 111th Street, Aslip, Illinois 60803

directions

From the center of Chicago, take I-55 South for more than 6 miles to Exit 286, Cicero Avenue. Turn left onto Cicero Avenue and follow it for almost 7 miles before turning right onto West 95th Street. Follow West 95th Street for 2 miles and then turn left onto Ridgeland Avenue. After 2 miles, turn left onto West 111th Street. The cemetery will be on your right.

history

After World War I, this cemetery was one of the forerunners of the modern cemetery. Upkeep of plots was, for the first time, guaranteed indefinitely. This cemetery was also the first in the area to offer headstones that did not stand, but were instead laid flat across the ground. Famous people from the area, such as Mayor Richard Daley and baseball umpire Stephen Cusack, are buried in this cemetery.

In the early 1930s, a local girl began to garner a reputation as a miracle healer. She was very religious, and people around the area would come to her hoping for some sort of miracle cure for their sickness. Tragically, the girl, named Mary Alice Quinn, died in 1935 at the age of 14. Knowing her reputation throughout the area and knowing that people seeking her help would flock to her grave and perhaps desecrate it looking for souvenirs or relics, her parents buried her in secret, in an unmarked grave within the family plot in section 7 at Holy Sepulcher Cemetery.

The plan did not work. People flocked from all over the world to the unmarked plot, digging up the ground to have dirt from her gravesite or leaving prayer books and rosaries. Still more people from around the world reported having visions of the girl and, as a result, went on pilgrimages to the cemetery to see her grave. Eventually, she was given her own stone.

Many people attribute miraculous healings to having visited the grave of Mary Alice Quinn.

ghost story

A young couple gave birth to a baby that was struck with a terrible illness. The doctors told the parents that the child would not live to see its first birthday. Unwilling to give up on their baby, the parents decided to bring it to the grave of Mary Alice Quinn. They laid the baby on the grave and were suddenly overcome by the smell of fresh roses. The baby got better and has not been sick since. The parents called it a miracle.

Others have experienced the smell of fresh roses when walking near the grave of Mary Alice Quinn. Others have reported actually seeing the ghost of the little girl. The ghost is said to appear in the form of a white mist or figure, which hovers over the top of the girl's headstone.

visiting

You may only enter the cemetery during regular business hours. It is open 8:30 a.m.–7 p.m. in the spring and summer, and 8:30 a.m.–5 p.m. during the fall and winter. All of the paranormal activity in this cemetery is reported during these hours, mostly when the sun is shining at its brightest, so these hours are by no means limiting. Do not remove anything from the grave of Mary Alice Quinn.

MOUNT CARMEL CEMETERY

1400 South Wolf Road, Hillside, Illinois 60162

directions

From the center of Chicago, take I-290 West for about 13 miles to Exit 16, Wolf Road. At the end of the exit ramp, turn left onto South Frontage Road. Take your first right onto Harrison Street. Follow Harrison Street for about 0.5 mile before turning left onto South Wolf Road. The cemetery will be on your right. The haunted section of the cemetery is through the front gate and to your left.

history

The cemetery was consecrated in 1901 and has seen more than 225,000 burials since that time. There are more than 400 private mausoleums in the cemetery. This cemetery is also the final resting place of many of the area's bishops, archbishops, and even a cardinal.

When you consider the ghost activity here, you may think that some of the cemetery's other residents may have something to do with it. Mobsters and crime lords, including Hymie Weiss, Dean O'Bannion, Frank Nitti, Vincent Drucci, and the Genna Brothers, are all buried here. They are buried alongside perhaps the most famous mobster of all time, Al Capone, whose marker bears the simple epitaph, "My Jesus Mercy."

Remarkably, the ghost stories at this cemetery don't have anything to do with these dark figures from Chicago history. The ghost stories are about a young woman named Julia Buccola Petta. In 1921, at the age of 29, she passed away. Her mother was distraught and had a marker built for her daughter that not only had a statue of a bride, but also a photograph of her daughter in her wedding dress. Six years passed with Petta peacefully resting beneath her magnificent marker. Then, Petta's mother started having dreams. In these dreams, Petta would come to her and tell her that she was still alive. These dreams haunted Petta's mother, and she was eventually able to secure permission to exhume her daughter's grave.

When they dug up Petta's grave, they discovered that the coffin had begun to rot away. Petta had not decayed at all, though. She appeared the same as she had on the day that she died. Her mother took a photograph of the pristine body. The photograph of Petta, six years dead, was placed on the grave marker next to the photograph of Petta in her wedding dress.

ghost story

It seems that having been exhumed and photographed has upset young Julia Petta. Since the time of the exhumation, ghost stories have been circulating throughout this cemetery about her. People often report seeing a young woman in a white wedding dress walking around the cemetery near Petta's grave. Many times, those who see her will describe the dress as having a glowing or ethereal look to it. When this strange figure is approached, it either slowly fades into nothingness or vanishes in a blink of an eye. Those who look at the photo of Petta on the gravestone know that the figure that they saw was Petta.

visiting

In order to find this ghost, you would have to enter the cemetery during normal business hours. The cemetery is open 8:30 a.m.–7 p.m. daily. Do not attempt to enter the cemetery after 7 p.m. You will be arrested. In order to find the ghost here, you will first have to find Julia Petta's grave. It's located at Section A, Block 6, Lot W2, Grave 5.

MT. THABOR CEMETERY

5313 Mt. Thabor Road, Woodstock, Illinois 60098

directions

From the center of Chicago, take I-90 West for a little more than 45.5 miles to the IL-47 exit toward Woodstock. Follow IL-47 for about 8.5 miles to IL-176. Turn right onto IL-176 and follow that for about 1 mile before turning left onto Mt. Thabor Road. The cemetery will be on your right.

history

The property was originally owned by a man named Owen Dyer in the early- to mid-1800s. In 1846, Dyer sold an acre of his land to the Catholic church for $1. The Catholics erected a church on the property known as the "Little Church in the Bush." As people in the parish began to die, the churchyard was used as a graveyard to bury locals in consecrated ground.

Eventually, the church fell into disuse and disrepair, and it was subsequently torn down. A large cross in the center of the cemetery marks where the church once stood. As of 1890, the cemetery fell into disuse, as well, due to its remote location. For a brief period of time in the 1960s, though, the cemetery was used to bury area babies who had died.

Since the cemetery is so remote, it became a magnet for vandals. Many times during the 20th century, the cemetery fell victim to their activity.

ghost story

At night, the cemetery is sometimes slowly overtaken by a thin green mist. Whenever this green mist overtakes the cemetery, people see shadowy figures walking through the mist. As the mist fades away, the figures are nowhere to be found.

Also at night, people witness balls of red, green, and white light floating through the cemetery. Sometimes, these balls of light appear in photographs, and other times, people see them with their naked eyes.

During the day, people feel cold spots manifest throughout the cemetery for no reason, even on the hottest of days. Witnesses also smell perfume throughout the cemetery.

visiting

There are no signs stating when the cemetery closes, and the gates are always open. Due to the instances of vandalism in this cemetery's past, though, you may want to stay out of the cemetery after dark so that passing law enforcement does not get the wrong idea about your intentions. This is OK because many of the phenomena found inside this cemetery—the cold spots and perfume smell—happen during the day. The other ghostly happenings usually are seen by passing cars at night. Feel free to drive by the cemetery all night long, or even park next to the cemetery and look inside from outside the gates.

NAPERVILLE CEMETERY

705 South Washington Street, Naperville, Illinois 60540

directions

From the center of Chicago, take I-290 West for a little more than 13.5 miles to I-88 West. Follow I-88 West for 7.5 miles to I-355 South. Take I-355 South for a little more than 3 miles and take the Maple Avenue exit. Keep right on the exit and merge onto Maple Avenue toward Naperville. Follow this road for almost 5 miles and turn left onto Washington Street. The cemetery will be on your right.

history

Whenever the words "ghost" and "Naperville Cemetery" are mentioned in the same sentence, locals immediately say the name Hillegas. Charles Hillegas and his wife (either Sarah or Jessie) were by all accounts incredibly happy together. Unfortunately, though, in the midst of this happiness, tragedy struck. Mrs. Hillegas fell ill and died. Here is where the two accounts of the story begin to diverge.

One account of the story states that she died in 1898. The other states that she died of influenza in 1912. Either way, Charles was heartbroken and had her body buried in Naperville Cemetery. It is here that the story becomes even darker.

According to one version of the story—the version printed the next week in the local newspaper—Charles began screaming that she was still alive as the casket was being lowered into the ground. Charles's concerned friends took him home and kept careful watch over him. A week after the body had been buried, he managed to slip away to the cemetery. He dug up the remains of his wife and took her home. His friends attempted to talk sense into him, but Charles armed himself and hid out in his barn to protect his wife's remains. Eventually, the sheriff captured him. His wife was returned to the cemetery, and he was sent to a mental institution.

While the above version of the story is what was reported in the local papers at the time, most people in Naperville know a different version of the story. Charles was an amateur chemist and, after the loss of his wife, he worked to develop a 'potion' to bring her back from the dead. Years after her burial, he felt that he had succeeded and went to the cemetery and dug up his wife. He gave her the formula.

The story goes on to say that he lived in his house with the corpse of his wife for two weeks before someone found out.

ghost story

Mr. and Mrs. Hillegas are buried in Naperville Cemetery. Perhaps they are one of the reasons for the plethora of ghosts that have been seen in the cemetery. The most often-seen ghosts take the form of glowing orbs of light. The orbs can be any variety of colors and sometimes even blink on and off. The blinking orbs have been seen so often that they have gained the nickname, "the hide-and-go-seek lights."

Beyond the lights, there are several apparitions that are seen throughout the cemetery. People sometimes see an old woman in the cemetery who disappears when approached. When it snows, people sometimes see the apparition of an older woman walking barefoot through the snow. Sometimes, people who enter the cemetery find bare footprints in the fresh snow and question why anyone would walk in the freezing snow in their bare feet.

Another menacing figure who is seen throughout the cemetery is known as the "shadow man." Many people see an imposing shadowy figure of a man who instantly vanishes upon being sighted.

visiting

The cemetery is open 9 a.m.–5 p.m. daily. This means that while you can enter the cemetery and search for the apparitions during the day, you will have to search the cemetery from outside the gates to watch for the hide-and-go-seek lights at night. The best time to search for the old woman apparition is early in the morning after a fresh snow has fallen the night before.

OAK HILL CEMETERY AND THE DEMON BUTCHER

8928 West 131st Street, Palos Park, Illinois 60464

directions

From the center of Chicago, take I-55 South for a little more than 13.5 miles to Exit 279 A-B towards La Grange Road. Take US-45 by taking the ramp on the left and follow this for a little more than 8.5 miles. Turn left onto West 131st Street and follow it for about 1 mile. The cemetery will be on your right.

history

In 1892 and 1893, as the World's Fair arrived in Chicago, some people opted to leave the increasingly crowded inner city and move to quieter, outlying areas. Particularly, a man named Hermann Butcher decided to move his butcher shop to the suburb of Palos Park in 1892.

For a few years, he ran his butcher shop successfully, but when The Great Depression hit, his business was affected. Despite his increasing troubles, he was the only butcher shop in town to stay open during the Depression. Butcher employed a young apprentice who everyone in town knew that he treated poorly. He would yell at the young man often and would overwork him constantly. One day, as the apprentice was carrying a load of meat down into the freezer, he fell and broke his neck.

Butcher, knowing that the town knew how he treated his apprentice, decided to hide the body in his freezer. Soon, people missed the apprentice around town. Butcher denied having seen him but knew that he had to get rid of the body. One day, as the meat was running short, he carved the leg of his apprentice and cooked and tasted it. He decided that it could pass for beef and displayed it in his shop. The town not only bought the entirety of the apprentice's 'meat,' but they came back begging for more.

Butcher decided that he had to provide for the town, so he would find hobos and small children in the area to lure back to his house to kill and butcher. Eventually, the townspeople began to suspect that he was to blame for the children who had gone missing in the area. They stormed the butcher shop and found a half-butchered 7-year-old in the basement. They then stormed Hermann Butcher's house and drug him out to the front lawn where they hacked him to death with his own butcher knives.

They cut off his head and buried it on Indian Hill. The rest of his body was later buried across the street at Oak Hill Cemetery.

ghost story

On Indian Hill there currently stands a preschool. Some people at the preschool report hearing what sounds like the clanging of knives from time to time within and around the school grounds.

The more famous ghost story in this area, though, is actually in some ways verifiable. The story goes that the demon butcher's body is attempting to reconnect with its head. The stories suggest that the grave of Hermann Butcher is actually moving toward Indian Hill, where his head is buried. This is actually documented and provable. The headstone itself is slowly creeping, year by year, across the cemetery grounds toward Indian Hill, which is across 131st Street from the cemetery. Experts say that the movement of the headstone is based on high water tables, causing the graves to become waterlogged, but they are unable to explain why the grave is moving toward the burial location of Butcher's head.

visiting

The preschool area is completely off limits. Indian Hill is privately owned and plays host to young children at a preschool. Do not, under any circumstances, step onto this property to search for ghosts. Oak Hill Cemetery, however, is open from sunrise until sunset. You can enter the cemetery grounds to find the grave of Hermann Butcher.

OAK WOODS CEMETERY

1035 East 67th Street, Chicago, Illinois 60637

directions

From the center of Chicago, take Lake Shore Drive to the south for about 5 miles to the 47th Street ramp. Turn right onto 47th Street and follow it for about 0.5 mile before turning left onto Woodlawn Avenue. Follow Woodlawn for another 2.5 miles before turning right onto East 67th Street. The cemetery will be on your left.

history

Oak Woods Cemetery is home to many famous people. Mayors of the city, as well as gangsters, Civil Rights activists, and scientists, are all buried here. One of the more famous burials is that of Olympic gold medalist Jesse Owens. The ghost stories about this place do not focus on any of these famous folks, though; they focus on a piece of ground within the cemetery known as the Confederate Mound.

During the Civil War, one of the worst prison camps in American history was in Chicago and was called Camp Douglas (see Camp Douglas chapter). Poor conditions led to many Confederate POWs dying within the camp. Many died of disease. Some died from escape attempts or even starvation. By the end of the war and the closing of the camp, thousands upon thousands had died on this site.

Many of those who died here were buried in the Old North Side Cemetery. But when the city cemetery closed, the bodies of the Confederate dead were moved to other cemeteries throughout the city, including Rosehill and Graceland. The most significant number of dead were moved to Oak Woods Cemetery. At least 6,000 Confederate dead are buried around the central monument on the Confederate Mound. This is the largest collection of Confederate dead in the North.

ghost story

The cemetery is haunted by the ghosts of the soldiers that are buried here. People see men dressed in either Union or Confederate Civil War uniforms walking through the cemetery. These apparitions are most often seen near the Confederate Mound. These apparitions mysteriously vanish soon after they are first seen.

People also hear screaming coming from the cemetery during both day and night. Those who investigate the screams never find any source for them. Strange lights have also been seen throughout the cemetery at night. These balls of light are said to float through the cemetery, then suddenly blink out.

visiting

The cemetery is open 8 a.m.–5 p.m. Monday–Saturday, and 9 a.m.–4 p.m. Sunday. You will be unable to enter the cemetery outside of these hours. The apparitions are most often seen within the cemetery during the day, so you can enter and look for the apparitions during regular hours. However, the screams and lights are most often experienced at night, and you will have to look for them from outside the cemetery gates.

QUEEN OF HEAVEN CEMETERY

1400 South Wolf Road, Hillside, Illinois 60162

directions

From the center of Chicago, take I-290 West for about 13 miles to Exit 16, the Wolf Road exit. Turn left onto South Frontage Road and then take a right onto Harrison Street. After a little less than 0.5 mile, turn left onto South Wolf Road. The Queen of Heaven Cemetery will be on your right after a little less than 1 mile.

history

Two historical events seem to affect the paranormal activity at this cemetery. One event is tragic, while the other is uplifting.

On December 1, 1958, shortly before classes let out for the day, a fire broke out at the foot of a stairway in Our Lady of the Angels School in Chicago. While the school was officially in compliance with fire codes of the time, it was still somewhat of a death trap for those caught inside during the fire. There was only one fire escape and few exits from which people could escape. The second-floor windows were a full 25 feet from the ground. Many people were trapped and killed inside of the building. Many more were injured or killed from jumping out of the second-story windows. All told, 95 people were lost in the fire. Of those killed, 92 of them were children at the elementary school. The victims of the fire were buried at the Shrine of the Holy Innocents at Queen of Heaven Cemetery.

The other story about the cemetery involves a man named Joseph Reinholtz, who was mostly blind. He went to Bosnia Herzegovina to visit a Virgin Mary apparition site and, upon returning home, was again able to see. He went back to the site in Bosnia and spoke to a visionary there named Vicka, who told him to go home and find a large crucifix by a three-branched tree to pray. Joseph found a crucifix that matched the description in the Queen of Heaven Cemetery.

For two years, Joseph prayed at the crucifix until, on August 15, 1990, the Virgin Mary appeared to him there. On November 1, the Virgin Mary appeared to him again, along with four angels. For a while, Joseph would experience the apparitions almost daily and reported to have seen apparitions of Jesus and Saint Joseph as well.

Since this time, the cemetery has become a pilgrimage site, where more than 11 million people have come to try to experience the holy apparitions themselves. The Catholic church has not yet designated the location as an official apparition site.

ghost story

Besides the apparitions of the Christian figures that have been reported at the crucifix, several other strange things have reportedly happened at Queen of Heaven Cemetery since Joseph first saw the apparition in 1990. The hands and feet of the crucifix have reportedly bled in front of witnesses. Witnesses will smell a strong scent of roses when they are in the vicinity of the crucifix, even in the middle of winter and despite no roses being close by. Another strange occurrence involves a rosary turning to gold.

There are also strange things that happen at the Shrine of the Holy Innocents. People report hearing the voices of small children, as well as crying. Others say that they see strange balls of light floating around the shrine. Some have captured these balls of light on film.

visiting

While Joseph Reinholtz saw apparitions at this site quite often, he strangely never experienced the apparitions or any other strange events on Tuesdays. If you go to the cemetery, you may want to avoid going on Tuesdays because, apparently, this is the day when you are least likely to experience something paranormal. The cemetery is open from sunrise until sunset daily. Make sure to exercise proper respect when walking onto the cemetery grounds because this is a sacred place. The crucifix is still at the cemetery, but its feet have been vandalized. Joseph Reinholtz is buried in the cemetery, as well, with the inscription, "Holy Mary Mother of God Pray for Us."

READ DUNNING MEMORIAL PARK

6596 West Belle Plaine Avenue, Chicago, Illinois 60634

directions

From the center of Chicago, take I-90 West for about 7.5 miles to Exit 43C, the Montrose Avenue exit. Turn left onto West Montrose Avenue and follow it for about 2.5 miles. Turn left onto North Narragansett Avenue and follow this for about 0.5 mile before turning right onto West Belle Plaine Avenue. Follow Belle Plaine Avenue until it turns sharply to the left. The memorial grounds will be at the corner on your right.

history

In 1851, construction began on the Cook County Insane Asylum or Read Dunning Insane Asylum on Oak Park Avenue. The asylum was a massive structure that dominated the area. Thousands upon thousands of people entered its doors. The asylum not only housed the insane from the Chicago area, but also was used to house sick and disabled people, the poor, and orphans. Many of the people who were housed at the asylum were treated poorly, and many died here and were buried at the cemetery that was on the asylum grounds. Many estimates state that more than 40,000 people were buried in this asylum cemetery.

Eventually, the asylum was moved and the old massive building was razed. The land was left vacant for some time until, in 1989, a shopping complex called Dunning Square was built on the site. Construction crews started digging up the land and were shocked to discover piles of bodies. It was quickly determined that they had come across the asylum cemetery grounds, so as many bodies as they were able to dig up were moved to the current site of Read Dunning Memorial Park.

The bodies were reburied in mass graves marked by the type of person that they were burying. One marker marks the burial location of orphaned children. Another marks victims of the Chicago Fire. Still others mark graves for the sick and the insane.

ghost story

Some people who enter these memorial grounds feel uncomfortable or feel like they are being watched. Others think that they hear footsteps approaching from behind them or hear the distant laughing of children.

Ghosts are also often seen at the memorial grounds. People see white transparent specters throughout the park. The most often-seen specter in this place is that of an elderly woman who is wearing a white hospital gown. Those who see her immediately know that she is a ghost because they are able to see through her. Those brave enough to approach witness her slowly fade away into nothingness. While the old lady in the gown is the most commonly seen apparition, other ghosts wearing similar white hospital gowns are seen roaming through the memorial grounds at all hours of the day and night.

visiting

This park closes at dark, although there are no signs that post hours at the gates. This is OK because the specters are seen during the day as well as at night. Furthermore, you are able to see into the park from outside the gates at night. When the specters appear at night, they will often have a soft white glow, so they are visible from outside the gates.

RESURRECTION CEMETERY

7200 Archer Road, Justice, Illinois 60458

directions

From the center of Chicago, take I-55 South for a little more than 10 miles until you get to Exit 282, IL-171 South towards 1st Avenue. Follow IL-171 for about 1.5 miles before merging to the right onto Archer Avenue. Follow Archer Avenue for about 2.5 miles. The cemetery will be on your right.

history

A small, unassuming headstone in Resurrection Cemetery holds the name Mary Bregovy. She died in an automobile accident in 1934. The world knows her as Resurrection Mary.

Mary was at the Oh Henry Ballroom (see Willowbrook Ballroom chapter) with her boyfriend when they got into a fight. It was a cold, dark night, but Mary was so upset that she opted to storm out of the ballroom and face the freezing walk home. She walked out onto Archer Avenue. Not far down the street, a car hit her. She fell to the side of the road. Had the driver stopped, she may have gotten to the hospital in time, but the driver drove on. Mary died from her injuries and the cold.

Her parents, worried since she had not arrived home, went out looking for her. They came across her body beside Archer Avenue. They were completely distraught.

They decided that they would bury her in her beautiful white dancing dress and shoes because she had loved dancing so much.

ghost story

Perhaps the most famous ghost in the Chicagoland area is that of Resurrection Mary. While phantom hitchhikers have become somewhat of an urban myth throughout the country, the legend seems to have started here, and upwards of 50 documented cases of her appearance have only bolstered the legend over the years.

As early as the 1930s, men have reported seeing a woman in a white dress walking alongside Archer Avenue between the Willowbrook Ballroom and Resurrection Cemetery. Sometimes these men will pick her up because it's cold outside and she seems upset. Other times, she will be hitchhiking, so they will stop to pick her up. She is always described as a beautiful young woman with blonde hair and blue eyes. She is always wearing a white dress, dancing shoes, and will often be carrying a small purse.

The men will pick her up and begin driving down Archer Avenue. At Resurrection Cemetery, she will be asked to be let out. Sometimes she will get out of the car and walk into the cemetery and vanish. Other times, she will vanish from the car, the door never having opened at all.

While Resurrection Mary is the most famous and most prolific ghost of the cemetery, there are other less popular stories that are told about the cemetery. People have seen and heard a horse-drawn carriage pull up to the cemetery gates. Figures are seen in the cemetery. For a while around August of 1976, there were rumors that two handprints that appeared burned into the iron gates were made by Resurrection Mary herself. Skeptics stated that the handprints were made by a truck that had veered off the road and into the gates.

visiting

The cemetery is open 8:30 a.m.–7 p.m. during the summer and the spring, and 8:30 a.m.–5 p.m. during the fall and the winter. This is OK, though, because the most famous ghost story does not involve going inside the cemetery at all. All you need is to, on a quiet night, drive the stretch between the Willowbrook Ballroom and Resurrection Cemetery. If you see a hitchhiker with a white dress, it may just be Resurrection Mary. The stories about Resurrection Mary are always told when the driver is alone, so you may not want to bring your friends along when trying to pick up this ghost.

RIVER VALLEY MEMORIAL GARDENS

14N689 Illinois Route 31, Dundee, Illinois 60118

directions

From the center of Chicago, take I-90 West for 27.5 miles until you get to the IL-31 North exit. Take IL-31 North for a little more than 0.5 mile and River Valley Memorial Gardens will be on your right.

history

The haunted history of this place doesn't really involve the cemetery itself but a house that once sat near IL-31, which, at the time, was between cemetery property and the road. In March 2003, the house was owned by a 32-year-old woman named Lynn Weis. On March 16, Lynn picked up a hitchhiker at Tollgate Road and drove her past her house toward East Dundee. Along the way, she made the mistake of pointing out her house to the hitchhiker, a woman named Vivian Mitchell.

Later that night, Mitchell returned to her house and broke in. She attacked Lynn with a hammer before stabbing her more than 90 times. In an attempt to cover up the murder, Mitchell set fire to the house, burning it to the ground. Firefighters determined that the fire was set at the foot of the bed where Lynn's body had been placed. Mitchell was eventually caught for the crime and was convicted. She was found guilty of the murder but, since she was mentally ill, received a sentence of life in prison rather than the death penalty.

ghost story

In general, the cemetery has a very tranquil atmosphere. Throughout most of the cemetery, there are no negative vibes or any paranormal indication that anything dark ever happened within these grounds. Compared to most cemeteries, this place actually has less of a feel of death and depression than most. The only exception to the peaceful atmosphere that encompasses this place is the small tract of land between IL-31 and the cemetery office where Lynn's house once stood.

Today, there is a metal door on the ground, which marks the place where the house once stood. People who tread in this area tend to get a completely different feeling than in the rest of the cemetery and will often experience other strange occurrences. Some experience ghostly smells. People smell what seems to be burning wood, perhaps remnants of the fire that took the house that once stood here. Others hear sounds. People have reported screams that seem to come from all around them. Still others have seen strange lights in the area where the house once stood. These lights have even been captured from time to time in photographs. Remnants of that terrible night when Weis was killed seem to echo in this unassuming corner of River Valley Memorial Gardens.

visiting

In order to actually stand in the area where the murder took place and where the house once stood, you will have to enter the cemetery during normal business hours. During the summer, these hours are 8 a.m.–7 p.m. During the winter, it is open 8 a.m.–5 p.m. Because the house once stood so close to the public road, you can still look and listen after dark from the adjacent road. As long as you don't enter cemetery property, you can still take pictures of the area while looking for strange lights or bring recorders to capture distant screams.

ROSEHILL CEMETERY

5800 North Ravenswood Avenue, Chicago, Illinois 60660

directions

From the center of Chicago, take North Lake Shore Drive for about 6 miles until you reach North Ridge Avenue. Turn right onto North Ridge Avenue and follow it for a little more than 0.5 mile. Turn left onto North Ravenswood Avenue. The cemetery will be on your right.

history

The cemetery was chartered in 1859, so it is one of the oldest non-sectarian cemeteries in the city of Chicago. The land for the cemetery was bought from a man named Hiram Roe under the condition that the cemetery created on the site be named after him. To honor this request, the cemetery was named Roe's Hill. An error made by a city clerk would soon change the name of the cemetery to Rosehill.

    Many notable Chicagoans are buried in this cemetery. Hertz, of car rental fame, as well as Montgomery Ward, Oscar Mayer, and department store magnate Richard

Sears, are all buried here. Bobby Franks, the murder victim of Leopold and Loeb, is also buried in a small mausoleum here, along with his father, Jacob Franks.

In 1885, a wealthy and important real estate tycoon named Charles Hopkinson died, and in his will, he had detailed plans for a tomb for himself and his family. The tomb would take the form of a small cathedral. Many of the owners of the grave plots behind the Hopkinson's plot were upset about the planned cathedral because it would likely block the views of their own tombs. The families took the Hopkinson family to court in a case that eventually ended up in the Illinois Supreme Court. It was ruled that the cathedral could indeed be built because the other families should have known that something could block the views of their own sites. The cathedral was built soon after.

ghost story

Rosehill Cemetery is filled with ghost stories. Every corner of the cemetery seems to have its own eerie tale to go along with it. Perhaps the most famous story involves the tomb of Charles Hopkinson. There are many reports that on the anniversary of Hopkinson's death, January 7, many strange sounds can be heard from the small, cathedral-shaped tomb. People will report moaning and the rattling of chains coming from the tomb. While this is most often reported on January 7, people have experienced this during other times of the year as well.

Another story involves a ghost that appeared to an employee near the Peterson Avenue wall of the cemetery. The employee saw a woman standing near this wall after the cemetery had closed, and walked over to ask her to leave. As he approached, he noticed that she was floating above the ground. She then began to fade away and disappeared into a cloud of slowly dissipating smoke. The story goes on to say that the next day, a young woman called to report that her aunt had appeared to her in a dream and that she wanted to add a marker to her aunt's unmarked grave. Remarkably, the unmarked gravesite was right where the employee had seen the apparition the evening before. The grave was marked, and the apparition was never seen again.

Throughout the rest of the cemetery, there are too many apparitions and sounds that have been reported to document in this limited amount of space. The smell of flowers has been said to surround Lulu Fellows's grave, even in the dead of winter. People hear sounds and see apparitions near the grave of Frances Pearce, a strange monument that displays a statue of Frances and her infant daughter—who died within months of each other—encased in a glass box.

As you approach the Ravenswood entrance to the cemetery, you are greeted by an imposing gate shaped like a gothic church. The daughter of the designer of this gate died of pneumonia during its construction but would often play around the gate while it was being built. People will often report seeing a little girl playing around the top of the tower at night.

visiting

The cemetery is open 8:30 a.m.–5 p.m. Monday–Friday, and 8 a.m.–4 p.m. Saturday–Sunday. In order to see the ghosts and graves inside the cemetery, you would need to enter during these times. The girl who haunts the gate can be seen at any time of the night, since you are able to see the gate from Ravenswood Avenue even after the cemetery has closed.

ST. JAMES SAG CEMETERY

10600 South Archer Avenue, Lemont, Illinois 60439

directions

From the center of Chicago, take I-55 South for a little more than 18 miles to Exit 274, State Route 83 South toward Kingery Road. Follow this road for almost 4.5 miles and then turn left onto Archer Avenue. The church and cemetery will be on your right soon after the turn.

history

The church and cemetery are situated on a bluff that overlooks the nearby Illinois and Michigan Canal. The oldest burial in the cemetery was from 1818, making it one of the oldest gravesites in the entire Chicagoland area. In 1930, a Catholic priest built a log church on the bluff to cater to the spiritual needs of the predominantly Irish workforce, which was working on the nearby canal. The church was popular in the area and eventually raised enough money to build the limestone church that sits there today. The current version of the church was built in 1850.

ghost story

Secluded and slightly off of the main road, the cemetery imbues visitors with creepy feelings as soon as they first glimpse the old headstones. At night, visitors sometimes catch sight of a horse and carriage, which rolls up to the front door of the church. A woman exits the church and steps inside of the carriage. The carriage then slowly starts to roll toward the front gate of the church near Archer Avenue, but it vanishes before reaching the main road.

Strange voices and phantom balls of light are often heard and seen throughout the cemetery. The voices most frequently heard in the cemetery seem to be monks chanting in Latin, despite the fact that monks have never historically occupied this church.

The monks aren't only heard but are also seen. People see figures in brown robes and hoods roaming through the cemetery, especially at night. While some accounts can be discounted as hoaxes or figments of one's imagination, there is an account in which a police officer reported seeing the monks. The officer reported seeing exactly eight monks exit the adjacent woods and begin moving toward the church's rectory. The officer began following the monks, and they vanished.

visiting

The cemetery itself is only open from sunrise until sunset. This creates some inconvenience for us ghost explorers because most of the paranormal activity here is reputed to take place after dark. Do not, under any circumstances, enter this cemetery after dark! You will be arrested. Some of the activity is viewable from Archer Avenue, which is a public road that runs adjacent to the church and cemetery. The carriage is exclusively seen from Archer Avenue. The lights that float through the cemetery are visible from Archer Avenue, as well. Who knows, you may catch a glimpse of a phantom monk crossing the street on the way to his favorite haunt.

TYRELL ROAD CEMETERY

Tyrell Road (County Highway 59), Gilberts, Illinois 60136

directions

From the center of Chicago, take I-90 West for 40 miles to the Randall Road exit. Keep right on the ramp toward Gilberts and merge onto Randall Road. Follow Randall Road for about 1.5 miles before turning left onto IL-72/Higgins Road. Follow Higgins Road for another 1.25 miles and then turn left onto Tyrell Road. The cemetery will be on your right after 1 mile. It is about 1,000 feet south of the I-90 overpass.

history

Officially, the cemetery is known as St. Mary's Catholic Cemetery. It was established in 1841 by Catholics in the area. Gilberts was, at the time, a very rural area, mostly composed of farmland. The burials that took place here in the early days were for farmers who lived in the area and cultivated the land.

The cemetery was built upon a small, tree-dotted hill in a clearing. Today, the cemetery appears the same, positioned atop a small hill, surrounded by trees on three sides. The town of Gilberts itself is still somewhat like it was many years ago, when the cemetery was first established. The area is mostly rural, despite some nearby suburbs. There is still farmland in the area. The cemetery on Tyrell Road is also much like it was more than 170 years ago.

ghost story

The cemetery is guarded by a ghostly sentry. Those who walk into the cemetery during daylight hours often say that they feel a presence at the front gate that is watching over the cemetery. Some have actually seen the guardian. They report seeing an older man who stands by the gate of the cemetery holding a green lantern. Those who see him say that they get a peaceful feeling from him. They believe that he is watching over the cemetery to guard it against vandals or others who are up to no good there.

Besides seeing the man with the green lantern at the front gate, people sometimes also see a green ball of light floating through the cemetery at night. Perhaps this is the man with the green lantern walking through the cemetery to look for intruders.

visiting

The cemetery is open from sunrise until sunset. You are not allowed to enter the cemetery grounds after dark. People have felt the presence of the ghost during daylight hours, although he is never actually seen during the day. The figure is only seen at night near the front gate. You can drive the adjacent road at any time of night looking for the ghost who stands watch at the gate, or otherwise look for the green lights that float through the cemetery.

WHITE CEMETERY

26274 West Cuba Road, Barrington, Illinois 60010

directions

From the center of Chicago, take I-90 West for 26.5 miles to the Roselle Road exit. Follow North Roselle Road for about 4 miles and then turn right onto Baldwin Road. Turn left onto West Northwest Highway/US-14 West and follow that for a little more than 6.5 miles before turning right onto Cuba Road. The cemetery will be about 1.5 miles down the road on your left.

history

White Cemetery is one of the older cemeteries in the Chicagoland area. It was officially chartered in 1855, but there were likely many burials here before that time. Many of the area's original settlers are buried here.

White Cemetery remained a relatively unknown cemetery on the outskirts of the Chicagoland area for most of its existence. In the 1970s, the cemetery began to garner more attention. Perhaps due to its remote location, teenagers began to enter the cemetery at night and vandalize the headstones and grounds. This vandalism became so prevalent that newspaper articles were written about the sad shape of the cemetery and the vandalism that the local youths were causing.

Eventually, the cemetery was monitored more closely and the vandalism lessened considerably. Despite the issues with vandalism having been resolved, something inside still seems mad as hell.

ghost story

This cemetery is considered by many in the area to be the second-most haunted cemetery in the Chicagoland area after Bachelor's Grove Cemetery (See Bachelor's Grove Cemetery chapter). The most commonly reported activity in this cemetery involves strange globes of light. These globes of light float throughout the cemetery and sometimes even drift over the gates and across Cuba Road.

While these globes of light are eerie and unexplainable, the creepier stories involve figures that are oftentimes seen in the cemetery at night. These figures appear hazy and are seen by witnesses as reliable as police officers. This group of shadowy figures is often seen loitering in the cemetery after dark. Most of the time, the figures are standing near the fence by Cuba Road, watching cars pass by. Other times, the group is standing near a small grove of trees within the cemetery. Whenever the figures are approached, they vanish into thin air.

Nighttime is not the only time when people report strange things in the vicinity of the cemetery. Even during the day, people see shadows cast along the ground or along Cuba Road. These shadows appear to be two people holding hands. There is nothing there to cast the shadows.

visiting

White Cemetery is closely monitored at dark because of the vandalism that has occurred there in the past. The cemetery is closed from sunrise until sunset most of the time. Sometimes, during the Halloween season, the hours are even more limited, due to fears of vandalism from thrill-seeking teenagers. This is OK. Most of the ghostly activity that occurs at night can be seen from outside the cemetery gates, and the cemetery is open during daylight hours, which allows you to see the mysterious shadows of the couple holding hands.

WOODLAWN CEMETERY

7750 Cermak Road, Forest Park, Illinois 60130

directions

From the center of Chicago, take I-290 West for a little more than 8 miles to Exit 21B, the Harlem Avenue exit. Turn left onto Harlem Avenue and follow it for a little more than 1.5 miles, then turn right onto Cermak Road. The cemetery will be on your right after about 0.75 mile.

history

On June 22, 1918, at around 4 a.m., the wheel bearings box on the Hagenback-Wallace Circus train overheated. The train stopped to allow the box to cool and took the proper precautions to avoid an accident by lighting red lights to warn any oncoming trains that the circus train had stopped. A train approached that was driven by an engineer notorious for falling asleep on the job. Somehow, he did not see the stopped circus train and crashed into its rear while traveling at full speed.

The back three cars of the circus train were destroyed. Parts of the wreckage and the remains of the trains caught fire. Some of the victims who were not killed instantly in the crash were caught underneath burning wreckage and killed by the flames. Officials estimated that 86 people were killed in the accident.

Woodlawn Cemetery contains a mass grave for 56 of the victims of the tragedy. It is in a section known as the Showman's Rest. The Showman's Rest contains these 56 victims, as well as many other showmen and circus performers who have chosen to be buried there as well. Many of the headstones in the area do not have names. One states "Baldy." Another states "4 Horse Driver." Most of them state "Unknown Male."

The Hagenback-Wallace Circus missed one performance as a result of the accident. After the missed performance, the circus continued as scheduled. After all, the show must go on.

ghost story

A ghost story about this cemetery states that at night you can hear the distant cries of elephants coming from the cemetery. The strange thing about this ghost story is that there were no elephants killed in the train wreck, and no elephants were buried in the cemetery. The strange sounds could perhaps be explained by the cemetery's proximity to the Brookfield Zoo.

While the elephant sounds are the most often-repeated ghost story from the cemetery, people also report hearing distant circus music when they approach Showman's Rest. There is no explanation for the music, and there does not really appear to be a source for the music. It seems to emanate from all around.

visiting

Like many cemeteries, Woodlawn is only open from sunrise until sunset. During these hours, you can approach Showman's Rest to determine if you are able to hear the distant sounds of circus music. Outside of these hours, you can stop outside of the gates of the cemetery and listen for the distant cries of elephants; try to determine if they are coming from the nearby zoo or from a different place altogether.

SECTION II

bars and restaurants

AL CAPONE'S HIDEAWAY AND STEAKHOUSE

35W337 Riverside Drive, St. Charles, Illinois 60174

directions

From the center of Chicago, take I-290 West for 22.5 miles to I-355 South toward Joliet. Follow I-355 for a little more than 2 miles to the Army Trail Road exit. Keep right and merge onto Army Trail Road towards Bloomingdale. Follow Army Trail Road for about 14 miles to IL-25. Turn left onto IL-25. Take your first right onto Pearson Drive. Take your first right onto Weber Drive. Follow Weber for about 1 mile and turn left onto Villa Maria Road. Turn right onto Park Place. Park Place will change its name to Riverside Drive. The location will be on your left.

history

Al Capone's Hideaway and Steakhouse was originally a bar called Reitmayer's Beer Garden. It was built in 1917. Just as the business started becoming successful, Prohibition began, and it became illegal to sell alcohol. This did not deter the Reitmayers, though, and they began brewing their own beer in a hidden cellar. They turned the beer garden into a speakeasy. Beer would flow into the speakeasy through copper pipes that ran from their hidden cellar.

Running a speakeasy was not an easy task in the 1920s, especially when business owners did not purchase their alcohol from one of the gangs that was running Chicago at the time. Each gang thought that the Reitmayers were purchasing alcohol from their rival gang, so they would often threaten the Reitmayers. They would come in and take "free" samples of the alcohol. Bugs Moran owned a rival speakeasy just down the street from the Reitmayers.

After Prohibition, the bar stayed in business. It continued to operate until recently, when hard times forced a (hopefully temporary) closure.

ghost story

When the bar was still open, most of the ghostly activity occurred on the second floor of the building. There was a particular table at the restaurant where the place settings would become messed up during the night. All of the other tables would be arranged for closing time, but this particular table would feature silverware and napkins all askew, as if someone had broken in and messed up one place setting on purpose.

The swinging doors that sat between the bar and the restaurant on the second floor were said to swing open by themselves as if someone had walked through them—though no one had.

Today, people see figures looking out from the second-floor windows when the building is empty. Strange figures and sounds are often heard in the area surrounding the building. People hear footsteps and, sometimes, laughter and partying coming from inside the building.

visiting

It is very unfortunate that this location is now closed. This bar did a very nice job of creating the atmosphere of a speakeasy that made you feel like you were back in the 1920s. Hopefully it will reopen soon; there are rumors of the sort.

Until such a reopening occurs, your only chance of experiencing these ghosts is to do so from outside. You may discern those phantom footsteps or hear the party rousing indoors. Do not walk onto the property because this is still private. You'll have to listen for ghosts from the adjacent road.

BUCKTOWN PUB

1658 West Cortland Street, Chicago, Illinois 60622

directions

From the center of Chicago, take I-90 West for about 2.5 miles to Exit 48A, the Armitage Avenue exit. Take the first left onto North Paulina Street, and then turn left onto Cortland Street. The Bucktown Pub will be on your left.

history

Previously, the pub was owned by a man named Wally, who was hated by his employees as he was often verbally abusive to them.

In 1986, Wally unexpectedly killed himself. The bar was left to his widow, who began to run the bar. Soon after taking control of the bar, though, she sold it off. Some say that she sold it off because Wally was still there.

ghost story

When the new owners took over, they rearranged the interior. But they would return each morning only to find that everything had been moved back to its original location. Coasters, bottles, and glasses that had been moved mysteriously returned to their original locations. This happened so often that the new owners eventually just gave up, keeping the bar the same as when Wally ran the place.

The jukebox in the bar also seems to have a mind of its own. It is known to suddenly turn on by itself when there is no one anywhere near it. No explanation has ever been found for this phenomenon, although it happens so frequently that the employees have grown to expect it.

Objects will also sometimes move on their own, sometimes even violently flying through the air and across the bar. Those who knew Wally think that this is a sure sign that he is still in the bar because Wally often threw things to emphasize a point when he was angry.

Apparitions also haunt the bar. Employees often hear or see a visitor enter the bar, but when they turn to face the visitor, the figure vanishes.

visiting

The ghosts at the Bucktown Pub can only be experienced from within the building itself. This means that you must enter during regular business hours. The Bucktown Pub is open 3 p.m.–2 a.m. Sunday–Friday and 3 p.m.–3 a.m. Saturday.

CALIFORNIA CLIPPER

1002 North California Avenue, Chicago, Illinois 60622

directions

From the center of Chicago, take I-90 West for a little more than 1 mile to Exit 49B, the Augusta Boulevard/Milwaukee Avenue exit. Turn right onto North Milwaukee Avenue and follow it for a little less than 0.5 mile before turning left onto Division Street. Follow Division Street for another 1.5 miles before turning left onto North California Avenue. The California Clipper will be on your right at the corner of Augusta Boulevard.

history

Today, the California Clipper is a bar, but it has had a rather eclectic and somewhat tumultuous history. The building began as a movie theater when it was built in 1912. In 1918, when the troops began coming home from the battlefields of World War I, an influenza epidemic broke out across the globe that would eventually kill millions. The movie theater was shut down for public welfare, preventing large gatherings of people that could possibly spread the disease.

It is somewhat unclear what was housed within the building during the next decade or two. Many believe that the building housed a speakeasy during this time, but no records exist to confirm this. Baby Face Nelson, a famous crime figure from Chicago, was born just a block south of the theater in 1908, so it is possible that he visited the building when it was still a movie theater and when it was a speakeasy, if that story is true.

In 1937, a business called the Clipper Tavern occupied the space. This operation continued for many years, until it was sold and renovated in 1999. It then became known as the California Clipper.

ghost story

Management and employees at the California Clipper are well aware of the ghost that seems to haunt the building. During renovations that occurred to the building five or six years ago, management called a psychic in to tell them more about the ghost that they all had seen. The psychic found a picture from the time when the building was the Clipper Tavern and identified a young blond woman in the picture as the ghost who had been haunting the place.

This was not too difficult to believe because many people claimed to have seen her throughout the years. A woman in a white dress has haunted the California Clipper for many years. The most common places that the woman appears are in booths one and nine. She has also been seen in the women's restroom, as well as the stairs leading to the upstairs apartments. Many times, the woman in white is followed by a very strong perfume scent that will often remain in the area long after she has vanished.

visiting

You must be 21 years or older to even enter this building. The building is open late daily, 8 p.m.–2 a.m. Sunday–Friday, and 8 p.m.–3 a.m. on Saturday. Management and employees are aware of the ghostly rumors and have even posted their own ghost stories on the restaurant's website. If you talk to one of the employees when you go in, he or she will likely have a personal ghost story or two to tell you.

CIGARS AND STRIPES BBQ LOUNGE

6715 West Ogden Avenue, Berwyn, Illinois 60402

directions

From the center of Chicago, take I-55 South for a little more than 7 miles to Exit 285, the Central Avenue exit. Turn right onto Central Avenue and follow it for a little more than 0.5 mile before turning left onto Pershing Road. Follow Pershing for 1.5 miles and then turn right onto Oak Park Avenue. After a little less than 0.5 mile, turn right onto Ogden Avenue. Cigars and Stripes will be on your left.

history

Although Cigars and Stripes itself has only been around for about 10 years, businesses and bars have occupied this site for decades prior. About 30 years ago, a man was in a bar at the location when he suddenly suffered a heart attack in the entryway to the building. He collapsed to the ground, gripping his chest. He was dead before help could be summoned.

Cigars and Stripes features a hand-crafted bar originally built for the Stardust Lounge, which sits several blocks from Cigars and Stripes. The bar was built by a man named Joe for his wife, Rose, when they owned the Stardust Lounge. The bar was built with careful love and attention, and, although Joe and Rose are gone from the mortal world, the bar and, perhaps, their spirits remain.

ghost story

The bar has its share of typical barroom hauntings. Footsteps often echo down the basement steps, although no one is on the stairs. Lights flicker or turn on and off for no reason. Glasses often move of their own accord. Sometimes, they tip over. Other times, they slide across the tables. In one instance, a glass actually flipped over and landed upside down on the table, despite no one having touched it. Bottles and glasses have fallen from the shelves. Tables and chairs have moved on their own. Martini shakers have flipped through the air. The phone has moved by itself. All sorts of strange activity has been reported here.

Besides the plethora of paranormal activities that tend to happen in the bar, a host of other ghosts haunt this place. A woman is seen or felt at a table in the back of the building. She is an older woman, who is often seen or felt praying for the wellbeing of her family and friends. An apparition who appears as a black shadow without arms or legs will float down the hallway between the bar and the beer garden. Rose herself often appears at her favorite spot at the bar that was moved from the Stardust Lounge. She is a friendly ghost and will often play matchmaker between people who are sitting at the bar. One couple attributes their marriage to Rose, who introduced them one night at the bar.

visiting

The bar is open 1 p.m.–1 a.m. Sunday–Thursday, and 1 p.m.–2 a.m. Friday–Saturday. You may only enter the building during these hours if you hope to experience the ghosts. Sit at the bar and order a drink. If your drink doesn't fall over, perhaps Rose will introduce you to a person sitting on the other side of the room.

CLARK STREET ALE HOUSE

742 North Clark Street, Chicago, Illinois 60654

directions

From the center of Chicago, take LaSalle Street to the north over the Chicago River. Follow LaSalle Street for about 1 mile to West Chicago Avenue. Turn right onto Chicago Avenue and then take your first right onto North Clark Street. The Clark Street Ale House will be on your right.

history

Today, the Clark Street Ale House is one of Chicago's favorite bars and is considered by many of its regulars to be the definition of a Chicago bar. The staff is friendly. The eclectic beer selection includes 95 different varieties, and the patrons aren't pretentious or mean. Before the business was the Clark Street Ale House, it was known as the Stop and Drink Liquor House.

There was once a regular at this bar known as "Droopy." He would come to the bar with the sole intention of getting drunk and would drink himself into oblivion most every night. Often, Droopy would get so drunk that he would not be able to walk. Because he was such a good customer and so well-liked at the bar, the owner would usually let Droopy sleep it off on a cot in the basement of the building. But one morning, Droopy didn't wake up.

Today, the bar still has the death certificate for Droopy, one of their best and favorite customers.

ghost story

Those who know about the ghost here at the Clark Street Ale House often say that Droopy haunts the building. No one has ever seen him, but they all know the story about how he died in the building and just assume that the strange sounds they hear are the sounds of Droopy, who loved the bar as much as those at the bar loved him.

The second floor of the building is unused. No one lives or works up there, but when the bar is quiet, bartenders, and sometimes patrons, will hear what sounds like footsteps coming from upstairs. Most of the time they ignore the sounds, assuming that Droopy is up to his old tricks, but when they do go upstairs to investigate, they find the building to be empty.

Bartenders and employees report that, sometimes when they go downstairs into the basement, they hear the sound of footsteps coming from the main bar area. They go upstairs to advise whoever is up there that the bar is closed, but instead find the building empty and the doors locked.

visiting

The Clark Street Ale House is open Monday–Friday, 4 p.m.–4 a.m. On Saturday, it is open from 11 a.m.–5 a.m., and on Sunday, it is open 11 a.m.–4 a.m. The bartenders are all very friendly and will happily tell you about their own encounters with the ghost of Droopy, if you ask.

COUNTRY HOUSE RESTAURANT

241 55th Street, Clarendon Hills, Illinois 60514

directions

From the center of Chicago, take I-290 West for about 13.5 miles to I-88 West. Follow I-88 West for another 3.5 miles and exit onto IL-83 South. Follow IL-83 for 4.5 miles and take the 55th Street exit. Turn left onto 55th Street West. The restaurant will be on your left.

history

This restaurant was built in 1922 as a restaurant and residence. Throughout the early years of the restaurant, it changed ownership many times. The last time that the restaurant changed ownership was in 1974, when the building was renovated into the structure that currently stands today.

In the 1950s, a woman walked into the bar to speak with one of the bartenders. Apparently, they had been dating, and she needed him to watch her child for a little while as she ran some errands. The bartender refused, which sparked a fight.

Furious, the woman stormed out of the building, leaving her child there. The woman sped off and purposefully slammed her car into a tree about a half mile down the road, killing herself.

ghost story

At one point, the owners of the building were very frightened of the ghost that they were certain haunted their restaurant. They invited paranormal researchers and psychics into the building to determine what was haunting the building and how to get rid of the ghost. The researchers advised that the ghost was that of the young woman who killed herself after leaving the building. They were unable to get rid of the ghost.

At any time of the day or night, windows, shutters, and doors will open by themselves and violently slam shut for no reason. Sometimes, there is a pounding on the walls that, upon investigation, has no source. People hear phantom voices within the restaurant, even when it is empty. The sounds of a crying baby are also heard throughout the building, even when there is no baby there. Pots and pans clank together on their own accord and footsteps follow patrons and employees, despite no one being behind them.

It is rare that an apparition is seen within the building, but when people see the apparition, they describe her as a young woman who matches the description of the woman who killed herself. She is said to stand by the jukebox in the middle of the night and play music. She beckons to people outside of the building from an upstairs window. She stands in front of the women's restroom, blocking anyone from entering. Then, she disappears.

visiting

In order to experience the ghostly activity here, you must enter during normal business hours. The building is open 11–1 a.m. Monday–Thursday, 11–2 a.m. Friday–Saturday, and noon–1 a.m. Sunday.

THE DRINKINGBIRD

2201 North Clybourn Avenue, Chicago, Illinois 60614

directions

From the center of Chicago, take I-90 West for 2.5 miles to the Armitage Avenue exit, 48A. Take a sharp right onto Armitage Avenue at the end of the ramp, then take the second left onto North Ashland Avenue. After a little less than 0.5 mile, turn right onto North Clybourn Avenue. After about 0.25 mile, The Drinkingbird will be on your left.

history

The site where The Drinkingbird sits today was once a tavern owned by Adolph Luetgert. Many in the Chicagoland area are well aware of Adolph Luetgert's reputation and, as a result, many exaggerations and untruths have been told about the site of The Drinkingbird. The most famous story about Luetgert was that he owned his own sausage factory and killed his wife within the walls of it. Some say that The Drinkingbird was a butcher shop owned by Luetgert at the time of the murders, and that he made his wife into sausage and sold it to unsuspecting customers at this site. This is most likely fabricated, as are the stories that he killed his first wife and his children in the building.

Still, there are numerous other stories about the building, including possibly true tales of death and murder at this site. One story does involve Luetgert, from the time that he owned the tavern at this site. According to the story, there was a man who often walked by the tavern and spit his tobacco onto the sidewalk outside. Luetgert would warn the man repeatedly not to spit the tobacco on the sidewalk outside the tavern, but the man continued to do so. Finally fed up, when the man spit tobacco on his sidewalk again, Luetgert attacked him and shoved the tobacco down the man's throat, choking him to death. Some stories state that the tobacco was shoved down his throat with such force that the man's esophagus split.

Other stories about the site talk about tunnels underneath the site that were used in the 1960s for child prostitution. One particularly gruesome story notes that a young girl who was enslaved in the child prostitution tunnels was killed and hacked into 47 pieces.

ghost story

Most of the ghosts in the bar seem to be those of small children. People say that they hear the laughter of children and, sometimes, even the sobbing or crying of children inside the bar or in the hallways behind the bar. Others see shadows on the walls. Sometimes these shadows are those of grown men. Other times, these shadows appear to be those of small children, even when there are no children in the building.

Doors also open and close on their own. Glasses move by themselves, as do tables and chairs. One story holds that a paranormal investigator was at the site and was thrown back against the wall as his equipment malfunctioned. While Luetgert likely did not make his wife into sausage in this building, there does seem to be some kind of ghostly activity here.

visiting

In order to enter this haunted place, you will have to honor regular business hours. From Monday through Friday, it is open 5 p.m.–2 a.m. On Saturday, it is open 1 p.m.–3 a.m., and on Sunday, it is open 11–2 a.m. The tunnels that run underneath the building are closed to the public and are not accessible. Before the bar was The Drinkingbird, it was a bar called Flounders. When it was Flounders, the bar owners were all about the ghostly lore, but now that it is The Drinkingbird, they are more hesitant to discuss the ghosts that supposedly haunt the place.

EDGEWATER LOUNGE
5600 North Ashland Avenue, Chicago, Illinois 60660

directions

From the center of Chicago, take North Lake Shore Drive for 5.5 miles until you reach the Bryn Mawr Avenue ramp. Turn left onto Bryn Mawr Avenue and follow it for about 1 mile to North Ashland Avenue. The lounge is on the corner of Bryn Mawr and Ashland. If you turn right onto Ashland, it will be on your left.

history

The building that houses the Edgewater Lounge—just The Edgewater to some—has been around since 1901. The building first became a tavern in 1908, and has remained a lounge or a tavern since that time. During Prohibition, the building was a speakeasy that used an auto parts store as a front. While the auto parts store operated for all to see, alcohol flowed discreetly in the back.

The Lounge was first called the Edgewater around 1970, when it was owned by a woman named Mary. Mary ran the bar for about 25 years before deciding to lease it out and have someone else take over the responsibilities. The man that she chose to lease the bar to ended up being a bad choice. The man, McPartlan, removed all of the valuable bar fixtures, including the original Brunswick bar, and set the lounge on fire. But the fire did not take and only damaged the bar area. McPartlan fled and was never heard from again.

Eventually, the bar passed to different ownership and Mary passed away. Today, the lounge is a popular neighborhood hangout. According to those who work at the lounge, there are more spirits here than there is alcohol behind the bar.

ghost story

Most every employee of the Edgewater Lounge believes that the building is haunted. Perhaps it's just the feeling that some encounter when walking in. Perhaps it is because objects move across tables or appear in places they were not left. Perhaps it is because, on occasion, the owner of the building sees a figure standing by the first tap at the bar when the building is supposed to be empty.

The most famous ghost in the bar is that of its former owner Mary. Mary haunts the upper floor of the building. People hear footsteps upstairs and a female voice coming from above, even when there is no one on that floor. Others have actually seen Mary walking around on the second floor of the building, only to witness her vanish before their eyes.

visiting

Most of the people who work at the lounge know that it is haunted. If they are not too busy, they may be able to tell you a story or two themselves. Make sure that you enter the building only during regular business hours. It is open noon–2 a.m. Sunday–Friday, and noon–3 a.m. Saturday.

ETHYL'S PARTY

2600 South Wentworth Avenue, Chicago, Illinois 60616

directions

From the center of Chicago, take South State Street for about 2.5 miles to West 26th Street. Turn right onto West 26th Street and follow it for a little more than 0.25 mile to South Wentworth Avenue. Turn left onto South Wentworth Avenue and the bar will be on the corner on your right. There is no longer a sign in front of the bar, since a truck knocked it down several years ago, and they haven't gotten around to erecting a new one.

history

The building was constructed in 1908 as a funeral home. From 1908 until 1995, the building served the Italian community just outside of Chinatown. Throughout nearly a century of operation as a funeral home, countless bodies and countless mourners have passed through its rooms.

When the building became a bar called Tito's in 1995, many of the locals who knew the building's history were frightened to enter it. But in time, patrons came, and its past was forgotten by most. Still, employees would not enter the cold storage area in the basement because this was the room that was once used for embalming.

The current owners changed the name of the bar to Ethyl's Party after a homeless man that the owner often gave money to. The first day that the business was open, a man came in and robbed the place. As the story goes, he grabbed the money and began to run toward the exit, when he suddenly collapsed and died near the front door. The autopsy showed that he had died of a heart attack, even though he had been a young and healthy man with no sign of heart problems.

ghost story

Shadowy figures lurk throughout this bar quite often. Most of the time, people spot a figure out of the corner of their eye, but turn to face this figure only to find that there is no one there. The most frequently seen figure in the bar is that of an older man wearing a trench coat. The man is often seen near the stage area, which was used for wakes when the bar was a funeral home. The man is said to disappear without a trace.

People also often see strange clouds of smoke that almost materialize into figures as they float slowly across the bar. The clouds of smoke are quite hazy but suddenly become thicker and gain structure and form before again dissipating into nothingness.

Televisions in the bar mysteriously change channels without anyone touching the units or the remote. People hear voices directly behind them speaking their names, but they will turn around to find no one there.

visiting

In order to encounter these ghosts, you will need to enter the establishment during normal business hours. It is open 11–2 a.m. daily. There is not a specific time that is best for spotting ghosts here, but people tend to experience unexplained phenomena when there are not many other patrons present. Your best bet for seeing the ghosts would be to visit when the bar is not busy.

EXCALIBUR NIGHTCLUB

632 North Dearborn Street, Chicago, Illinois 60654

directions

This nightclub is in the center of Chicago, just north of the Chicago River. To get to it, take LaSalle Street north over the river to Ohio Street. Turn right onto Ohio Street and then left onto Dearborn Street. The nightclub will be on your left.

history

At 9 p.m. on Sunday, October 8, 1871, something caught fire in a barn behind DeKoven Street. The conditions were perfect for one of the greatest disasters in American history. The city of Chicago, at the time, was mostly constructed from wood. There had been a drought in the area, which made conditions incredibly dry. And Chicago's infamous wind was howling that night.

The barn blazed out of control, and flames soon leapt to the adjacent building. Additional buildings caught fire quickly. Soon, the heat from the fire caused more buildings to combust before the actual flames even reached them.

Because the fire moved so quickly and grew so widespread, people had trouble escaping the flames. Many were caught inside of buildings and burned to death. Others were killed in the streets as the heat of the flames and collapsing buildings overtook them.

Several women who were running to escape the flames decided to try to take refuge in a building that stood on the site where the Excalibur nightclub is today. It was a futile effort to survive. The flames soon engulfed the building, trapping them inside. They screamed for help as they burned to death.

ghost story

The women who died here during the Great Chicago Fire are said to haunt the building to this day. Candles are said to reignite after closing time. Drinking glasses and beer bottles sometimes crack or shatter for no reason. Alarms sound and, upon investigation, there is no one there to set them off. Employees hear people call their names, recognizing the voices as those of people who are out of town or deceased.

The women who burned to death here are seen and heard in the building. People hear panicked screams coming from the restrooms in the downstairs area of the nightclub, even when the restrooms are empty. A famous Polaroid photograph was taken of the nightclub in which a ghostly woman in a red dress is seen walking past one of the windows.

Many other strange things have been experienced within this building. Objects appear on ledges that are out of reach. For example, a teddy bear once was perched on a ledge that was 25 feet above the floor. Chairs and alcohol cases have stacked themselves, sometimes to towering heights, despite there being no nearby people or ladders.

visiting

If you're hoping to experience some of these strange happenings at the Excalibur nightclub, you will have to enter during regular business hours. It is open Tuesday–Friday 7 p.m.–4 a.m., and on Saturday 7 p.m.–5 a.m. If a nightclub isn't your scene, you can still take photographs of the windows from the outside of the building and perhaps capture a photo of the lady in red.

FIRESIDE LOUNGE

5739 North Ravenswood Avenue, Chicago, Illinois 60660

directions

From the center of Chicago, take North Lake Shore Drive for 5.5 miles to Bryn Mawr Avenue. Turn left onto West Bryn Mawr Avenue and follow that for another mile. Turn right onto North Ravenswood Avenue. The Fireside Lounge will be on your right. There is a parking lot directly adjacent to the lounge and Rosehill Cemetery is across the street.

history

The building that now houses Fireside Lounge was constructed in 1904 as both an inn and a tavern. The inn was most often used by mourners. Rosehill Cemetery is directly across the street from the building, so the inn became the perfect place for mourners from out of town to stay while they worked through their grief. Countless mourners spent tearful nights in the rooms that occupied the upstairs of the building.

While the lounge that occupies this site today no longer accepts lodgers for the night, some who have been here swear that lodgers from long ago still inhabit this place.

ghost story

Some of the most common ghost stories about this building state that items throughout the lounge move around on their own. Waitresses leave drinks or other items in certain places and then return to find that they have moved to entirely different places within the bar. There is no explanation as to why the items have moved. Other waitresses have reported watching items move by themselves. Salt or pepper shakers will fling themselves across the room at unsuspecting employees, and glasses will slide around on empty tabletops when there is no one nearby.

The most famous ghost in the building, though, is that of a young woman. The story says that the young woman came to stay at the inn every year on the anniversary of her husband's death to visit his grave at Rosehill. Now that she, too, has passed, her spirit is often experienced within the Fireside Lounge building. People who experience her say that they simply hear her footsteps on the second floor where she would stay each year. The footsteps tread back and forth and are heard even when there is no one on the second floor of the building.

visiting

In order to experience ghostly happenings at the Fireside Lounge, you must enter during normal business hours. It is open Monday–Friday 11–4 a.m., on Saturday 11–5 a.m., and on Sunday 10–4 a.m.

GOLD STAR BAR

1755 West Division Street, Chicago, Illinois 60622

directions

From the center of Chicago, take I-90 West for a little more than 1 mile to the Augusta Boulevard exit, 49B. At the end of the exit, take a right onto Milwaukee Avenue and follow this road for a little less than 0.5 mile to West Division Street. Turn left onto West Division Street. The Gold Star Bar will be on your left. It is not easy to find. It is next to a liquor store and has a façade consisting of plywood painted black. Gold Star Bar is painted in gold letters above the front door.

history

The neighborhood where the Gold Star Bar sits today is better than it once was. Once, there was a brothel housed in the upstairs of the bar. All sorts of unsavory characters would inhabit this bar. There would often be bar fights. Sometimes, these bar fights were rumored to have ended in death. The bar was a rough place, and dark things happened here.

In the 1950s, the area was exceptionally dangerous, and several holdups and robberies happened at this bar. The owner of the bar was unwilling to allow this to continue, however, so he armed himself. One day, a man walked through the front door of the bar and announced that he was armed and intended to rob the place. The owner of the bar took out his gun and shot the robber to death in the doorway.

ghost story

The front doorway of the bar carries a strange atmosphere. There are odd temperature fluctuations in the front doorway that cannot easily be attributed to exterior or interior temperatures. At times, it is warm both outside and inside the bar but completely freezing in the doorway. People also often feel very uncomfortable and nervous when they are standing in the doorway. As soon as they enter or leave the bar, though, these feelings instantly dissipate.

The interior of the bar seems to be haunted by two figures. One of them is an attractive young woman in a lime green dress. She looks like a real person until she vanishes in an instant, leaving witnesses wondering if they had even seen her in the first place. She is known at the bar as the Woman in Green, and she has been seen frequently throughout the establishment. Another ghostly figure who haunts the bar always takes the form of an older man wearing a straw hat. The straw hat makes him stand out in a crowd, but he, like the Woman in Green, is said to suddenly disappear as if he were never there.

visiting

The bar is open Monday–Friday 4 p.m.–2 a.m., and on Saturday 4 p.m.–3 a.m. If you wish to experience ghosts, this is the time you need to go. Although the neighborhood is much better today than it was when this bar housed many of the area's least savory characters, it is still not the best neighborhood in the city, and you should always remain vigilant.

GREEN MILL COCKTAIL LOUNGE

4802 North Broadway Street, Chicago, Illinois 60640

directions

From the middle of the city, take North Lake Shore Drive to the north for about 5 miles to the Lawrence Avenue ramp. At the end of the ramp, turn left onto West Lawrence Avenue. After about 0.5 mile, turn right onto North Broadway Street. The Green Mill Cocktail Lounge will be at the corner on your left.

history

The Green Mill Cocktail Lounge is one of Uptown's oldest bars. The bar first opened in 1907 as Pop Morse's Roadhouse before changing its name to Green Mill Gardens a couple years later. The name stemmed from that of the gardens that existed on the property until the early 1920s. The bar's early years, however, likely have little to do with its haunting. The dark history of this place is much more likely a result of Prohibition.

When Prohibition began, the bar fell into the hands of one of Chicago's most noted gangsters, "Machine Gun" Jack McGurn. McGurn was one of Al Capone's most trusted lieutenants, and he turned the bar into one of the more popular speakeasies in town. Underground tunnels provided a secret avenue with which to transport illegal alcohol into the building, as well as a secret place where the mobsters could carry out and conceal other crimes. Many murders likely occurred in these underground tunnels. A popular piece of gangland history involves the bar. McGurn wanted comedian Joe E. Lewis to sign a contract with the Green Mill, but Lewis refused, having been offered more money at a different bar that was run by the North Side Gang. McGurn had his men cut Lewis' throat in November of 1927 at the Commonwealth Hotel as a result of this refusal. Lewis survived, and Capone gave him $10,000 as an apology.

After Prohibition, the bar passed back to reputable hands, but it has retained the décor and mystique of the Prohibition-era speakeasy and jazz club that made it famous.

ghost story

Some bartenders and employees at the bar accept the ghosts as permanent fixtures— expected facets of this historic lounge. As bartenders open the bar in the morning, they sometimes hear piano playing coming from inside. Upon investigation, the building is found to be completely empty. Other times, drinks make themselves. Bartenders glance across the bar to see a freshly made drink by an empty seat. The bartenders are unable to come up with any explanations as to how these drinks appear.

Other ghost stories center around the basement, which was once part of the tunnels that were used to traffic alcohol during Prohibition, among other illegal and immoral activities. Down here, objects often move on their own accord. Employees descend into the basement expecting to find something where they left it, only to find that the item they are searching for has moved. Many times, these items move to the top shelf, which is only reachable by ladder. No one else with access to the basement will admit to having moved anything, and many of the employees here have had similar experiences.

visiting

In order to visit the Green Mill, you will have to enter during normal business hours. Monday–Friday, the bar is open noon–4 a.m. On Saturday, it is open noon–5 a.m., and on Sunday, 11–4 a.m.

Sit at the bar and watch for strange drinks that have made themselves, or watch the piano when there is no one around to see if it plays on its own. The basement storage area, though, is only accessible by employees, so you'll need to stay in the upstairs part of the bar.

HOOTERS ON WELLS STREET

660 North Wells Street, Chicago, Illinois 60610

directions

Hooters is near the center of Chicago, just north of the Chicago River. Take LaSalle Street to the north for a little more than 0.5 mile, then turn left onto West Erie Street. Follow Erie for one block, then turn right onto North Wells Street. Hooters will be on the corner on your left.

history

The late 1800s were the years of the Resurrectionists. Today, we refer to the Resurrectionists as grave robbers. In the late 1800s, the study of medicine was starting to move into the modern age. In order to study the inner workings of the human body, though, doctors needed cadavers. Originally, the only bodies doctors had access to were those of executed criminals. This created a need for bodies that was filled by these Resurrectionists. The Resurrectionists dug up bodies from their graves and sold them to medical schools throughout the Chicago area.

In 1875, the market for bodies in Chicago stopped as new laws enabled medical schools to use bodies that were otherwise destined for the potter's field. These were typically the bodies of persons too poor to afford graves in a regular cemetery.

While the demand for bodies disappeared in Chicago, Chicago still had plenty of bodies that the Resurrectionists could steal. Many surrounding cities in Michigan and Iowa still needed bodies for their medical schools because they had no such laws allowing harvest from the local potter's field.

Grave-robbing became a huge business in Chicago, and more bodies than ever were stolen from their graves. The Resurrectionists would dig up a grave, cut off the top of the coffin, and remove the victim's body from the ground with a large hook.

The Resurrectionists needed a place to store the bodies as they prepared them for transport to other states. The place they chose is the building where Hooters is today. All of the bodies were moved to the 600 block of Wells Street, where they were stored until they could be shipped to Michigan and Iowa. Hundreds, if not thousands, of bodies likely moved through this building.

Eventually, the Resurrectionists went out of business, as the demand for fresh corpses decreased. The building on Wells Street was home to many businesses that eventually moved out. Some say that those who ran businesses here were scared out by some otherworldly force. Eventually, the building was bought by Hooters, which occupies it to this day.

ghost story

Many strange things occur within this Hooters restaurant. Temperatures are said to drop dramatically for no apparent reason, in seemingly random places throughout the building. Objects suddenly fall off of tables or shelves within the building, even though no one has touched them. Battery-powered electronics seem to die more quickly within the building than at other locations, as if the building itself is draining the batteries' power. People see strange balls of light throughout the building that suddenly disappear. They hear footsteps in areas where no one is walking. The jukebox suddenly turns on by itself when there is no one nearby.

Some have seen apparitions of two different male ghosts and a female ghost within the building. They are dressed in 19th-century clothing and suddenly disappear upon being approached.

visiting

You must enter the building during regular business hours. It is open 11 a.m.–11 p.m. Sunday–Thursday, and 11 a.m.–midnight Friday and Saturday.

THE IRISH LEGEND PUB AND RESTAURANT

8933 South Archer Avenue, Willow Springs, Illinois 60480

directions

From the center of Chicago, take I-55 South for a little more than 13.5 miles until you reach Exit 279A-B, US-12, toward La Grange Road. Take US-12 East on the left side of the ramp and follow that for another 2 miles. At this point, merge onto Archer Avenue. After another 2 miles, you will see the restaurant on your left.

history

Much of Willow Springs was originally occupied by Native Americans and was considered sacred to those who lived there. Even decades later, residents still considered the land sacred, especially during the height of the Spiritualist movement.

The area's magical qualities only seem to have heightened the paranormal activity. During Prohibition, this place was a combination of a speakeasy and brothel. Al Capone was said to have visited this bar on several occasions, and there are rumors that many mob executions took place in the basement. There are also escape tunnels underneath the building that could have been used for quick exits from the bar in the event of a raid.

There are also stories about many abortions that took place in the basement of the building. When the prostitutes that worked upstairs became pregnant, they would simply go to the basement to have the children aborted.

ghost story

This bar sits across the street from the Willowbrook Ballroom, the last place where Resurrection Mary was seen alive. It also sits on Archer Avenue, perhaps the most haunted road in the Chicagoland area. It's no wonder that ghosts reside here.

Several ghost investigation groups have combed the building throughout its history, and several have come away with evidence of the paranormal. Most of this evidence comes in the form of Electronic Voice Phenomena (EVP). When the investigators review their audio recordings, they often hear strange voices or sounds that were not there at the time of the investigation. Other times, the investigator's electronic equipment malfunctions for no apparent reason, or the batteries on the equipment quickly drain.

Objects often move throughout the bar. Chairs fall over when there is no one nearby. Glasses and other items glide across tables, even when no one is touching them.

visiting

The Irish Legend is open 11–2 a.m. daily. If you wish to visit this haunted bar, you must enter during these business hours. Bring a recording device to try to catch some EVPs while sitting in the bar area, and wait for something to move, even if no one is touching it.

IVY

120 North Hale Street, Wheaton, Illinois 60187

directions

From the center of Chicago, take I-290 West for a little more than 13.5 miles to Exit 15A, I-88 West. About 0.5 mile farther, merge onto IL-38 West. Follow IL-38 for a little more than 10 miles and then turn right onto South Main Street. After about 0.5 mile, turn left onto West Liberty Drive, then take your first right onto South Hale Street. Ivy restaurant will be on your left.

history

This building was first constructed in 1928. It was originally a Catholic chapel. Later, it housed office supplies before becoming a funeral home. It continued as a funeral home for a while before numerous businesses moved in and out. Ivy finally took over the building in March 2009. The Ivy restaurant has had some success and seems to have some staying power.

Although the name of the restaurant clearly comes from the ivy-covered exterior walls, there are many stories that circulate about the building concerning a young girl who died here in the 1940s. Those who know of this young girl affectionately call her Ivy.

ghost story

The interior of this building is gorgeous and reminiscent of the Catholic chapel that once existed here. Arches and a stained-glass window create a breathtaking ambience that grabs you as soon as you step through the doors. Many a photographer has photographed the interior of the building, trying to capture the feeling that assails you as you enter. Some of these photographs contain more than what the photographer saw in front of him. Unexplainable fogs and strange balls of light tend to appear in photographs taken inside the restaurant.

The building is said to be haunted by two ghosts. The first ghost is that of a young girl. Those who have seen her have named her Ivy, thinking that she may be the ghost of the young girl who died in the building during the 1940s. Ivy is seen throughout the building and is somewhat ill-behaved. She is said to turn on water faucets in the upstairs bathroom and then vanish. People walking up or down the winding staircase see Ivy run by them on the stairs. When people follow after her, she is nowhere to be found.

The other ghost seems to be a caretaker of sorts for the young girl. The ghost is that of a well-dressed middle-aged man who is only seen at the same time as the young girl. He seems to be watching over her whenever he is seen. He dresses in 1940s clothing and disappears if approached.

visiting

The ghosts at this restaurant are experienced exclusively inside the building. To look for the ghosts, you must enter the building during normal business hours. Monday–Saturday, the restaurant is open 11–1 a.m.; Sunday, noon–11 p.m. There are both a restaurant and bar inside the building, so have a drink or two or stay for a meal.

LIAR'S CLUB

1665 West Fullerton Avenue, Chicago, Illinois 60614

directions

From the center of Chicago, take I-90 West for a little more than 3 miles to the Damen Avenue exit, Exit 47B. Turn right onto Damen Avenue and then take another right onto West Fullerton Avenue. The Liar's Club will be on your right.

history

Several murders have taken place in this building. Surprisingly, the murders all seem to have happened in the exact same place within the building. The first murder took place in 1958. A wife who had been abused by her husband had finally had enough. She attacked her abusive husband and killed him in a corner on the second floor of the building.

In 1968, the building was a homeless shelter. Two men were near the same corner on the second floor and got into a fight concerning a pair of pants. One of the two men grabbed a glass Coca-Cola bottle from the ground and beat the other to death in the corner.

The third murder occurred in 1986. At this point, the building was a tavern owned by a man named Frank Hansen. Frank lived in an apartment on the second floor of the tavern with his wife, Julia. The couple had serious problems and Julia had taken to verbally abusing Frank, often making fun of him for his small size. Finally, Frank retaliated by attacking her with an ax. He killed and dismembered her, leaving her body in the same ill-fated corner of the building for six days before he called the police to let them know what had happened.

ghost story

The second floor is haunted by the ghost of Julia Hansen. People report seeing a large woman on the second floor of the bar. Sometimes, she appears normal, but then she suddenly disappears. Other times, she is seen walking around without arms and with bloody ax wounds all over her body. These more frightening apparitions of Julia after the ax attack also disappear, but not before terrifying those who are caught by her alone on the second floor.

Many other strange things happen throughout the bar. A ghostly male figure has been seen walking up and down the stairs between the first and second floors. Upon reaching the top of the stairs, the man mysteriously disappears. Also, some people report feeling frightened and uncomfortable when they approach the upstairs corner where the three people were killed. It is said to possess a negative energy.

visiting

The second floor of the bar is open to the public, so you will be able to go up to the second floor in an attempt to find the ghost of Julia Hansen. The bar is open Monday–Friday 8 p.m.–2 a.m., and Saturday 8 p.m.–3 a.m. There is a $3 cover charge to get into the building.

METRO AND SMARTBAR

3730 North Clark Street, Chicago, Illinois 60613

directions

From the center of Chicago, take North Lake Shore Drive to the north for about 3 miles to the Belmont Avenue ramp. Turn left onto West Belmont Avenue and follow that for about 0.75 mile to North Clark Street. Turn right onto North Clark Street; the Metro and Smart Bar will be on your left.

history

This building was originally constructed on 1927 as a Swedish Community Center. But it changed hands several times before becoming the Metro venue it is today. Throughout its history, several women have died within this building's walls.

A cleaning lady named Marilyn, who worked in the building in the 1940s, was working late one night and decided that she would end her own life. She fashioned a noose and hanged herself from the ceiling on the fourth floor of the theater.

Another victim of the building was a young girl whose parents owned the building in the 1950s when it was a Swedish men's club. The girl quickly learned all the passages and ins and outs of the building and found her way to the top of the elevator, where she began playing. Unaware that her daughter was on top of the elevator, the girl's mother took the elevator up to the top floor. The small girl was crushed to death when it reached the top. (It should be noted that some accounts of this tragedy classify the young child as a boy.)

People say that there have been several other women who have met untimely ends here, but we were unable to unearth the details behind these other fatalities.

ghost story

Apparitions of those who have died are often seen throughout the building. The ghost of Marilyn is one of the most often seen in the building. She is always seen on the fourth-floor theater where she killed herself. Most of the time, her apparition is seen hanging by the neck and swinging from the rafters above.

The ladies' rooms in the building have their own share of strange apparitions. People in the restroom often see women suddenly vanish, and those in the bathroom stalls sometimes hear another enter and exit the stall next to them, but emerge only to find the bathroom empty.

The apparition of a very young boy, probably 2 or 3 years old, is also common. Strange lights sometimes appear throughout the building and slowly materialize into the form of this young boy. Some paranormal experts trace the activity within this building to an underground stream that runs beneath it. Some think that constantly running water is a catalyst for paranormal activity.

visiting

The Metro itself is only open during concerts. The concert schedule changes constantly, so you will need to check the website for up-to-date details. The Smart Bar is located on the bottom level of the building and is open Wednesday–Sunday. Wednesday–Friday and Sunday, the bar is open 10 p.m.–4 a.m. On Saturday, it is open 10 p.m.–5 a.m. If it is not convenient to attend a show, the bar is your best bet for experiencing a ghost here.

TONIC ROOM

2447 North Halsted Street, Chicago, Illinois 60614

directions

This location is just a couple minutes north of the center of the city. Start by taking North LaSalle Street for about 1.5 miles to West Division Street. Turn left onto West Division and angle to the right onto North Clybourn Avenue. Follow Clybourn for about 0.5 mile and turn right onto North Halsted Street. Follow North Halsted for about 1 mile. The Tonic Room will be on your right.

history

This site has a very tumultuous history. Starting in the 1920s, this building was a brothel and tavern, frequented by members of the Irish North Side Gang. Many dark and nefarious activities likely occurred within the building during these years. But the darker history could have very little to do with the gangsters that frequented this place in the 1920s.

Some say that the building was the secret meeting place of the American chapter of the Golden Dawn. The Golden Dawn is a secret society that uses ancient Egyptian iconography and practices as a pathway to knowledge. In the 1930s, a young girl accompanied her father to a meeting in the basement of the building. She claimed to have witnessed a human sacrifice.

In 1969, the building became a store called "El-Sabarum," which sold all manner of occult objects, including voodoo talismen and goat hooves. Eventually, the predominantly Christian neighborhood vilified the owner and the store, and he was forced to leave it.

When the owners of the Tonic Room took over the building, they were surprised by what they found in the basement. Egyptian symbols were painted all over the walls, and a large Pentagram was painted in the center of the floor.

ghost story

Many people feel an intangible and eerie sensation upon entering this building. Something will feel somewhat off and creepy about this place, but this feeling of discomfort is the least of the ghostly stories that circulate about this building.

People sometimes snap photographs within the building. These photographs often turn out strangely. Unusual mists or figures sometimes appear in the pictures. People, too, can appear distorted or blurry for no reason.

Employees and patrons alike also encounter apparitions throughout the building. The apparitions appear most often in the basement and to the employees, but they sometimes appear at the main bar as well. Perhaps these are the ghosts of deceased gangsters, or perhaps they belong to victims of the sordid acts that took place here.

visiting

The employees are well aware of the ghostly lore that surrounds their workplace and some even claim to have seen ghostly activity themselves. They won't mind if you go in for a drink and look for ghosts. The building is open during late hours. The doors open at 9 p.m. daily except Sunday, when it is closed. The bar closes at 2 a.m. Monday–Friday and 3 a.m. Saturday. Unfortunately, the basement is not accessible by the public, so you'll have to look for ghosts in the upstairs area.

WEBSTER'S WINE BAR

1408 West Webster Avenue, Chicago, Illinois 60614

directions

From the center of Chicago, take I-90 West for 2.5 miles to Exit 48A, the Armitage Avenue exit. Turn right onto Armitage Avenue and then take your second left onto North Ashland Avenue. After about 0.25 mile, turn right onto West Webster Avenue. After a little more than 0.25 mile, you will see Webster's Wine Bar on your left.

history

The building itself is more than 120 years old. It has had many uses throughout its long history, including an incarnation as a brothel, in which the first floor was used as a bar while the second was used for prostitution. There were no doubt countless other illegal activities taking place during this time.

Most recently, the building housed a fine art gallery until it was purchased in 1994, when a husband-and-wife duo turned it into a wine bar.

ghost story

Whatever ghosts may be in this building seem to be concentrated on the second floor. Employees and patrons have seen the apparition of a man who suddenly vanishes without a trace. Employees have heard footsteps coming from the upstairs, even when they were certain that no one was up there.

A local paranormal investigation group captured a strange voice via an audio recording that they made on the second floor of the building. Customers often say that they are unaware that the building is haunted, but that the atmosphere on the second floor is significantly different than that of the first floor. Customers sometimes state that they feel tense and uncomfortable while on the second floor, feelings that immediately dissipate upon returning to the first floor.

visiting

The building is open Monday–Friday 5 p.m.–2 a.m. On Saturday, it is open 4 p.m.–3 a.m., and on Sunday 4 p.m.–2 a.m. To experience the ghosts at this building, you will need to enter during regular business hours. The second floor is open to through traffic, and this is where most all of the ghostly activity is said to occur. The management of the building states that they have never experienced anything out of the ordinary in the building and they do not speak of any ghosts or rumors of ghosts in their building. If you enter the building to look for ghosts, it's probably best to head up to the second floor to grab a drink, not to ask anyone who works there about the ghosts that you hope to find.

WILLOWBROOK BALLROOM

8900 Archer Avenue, Willow Springs, Illinois 60480

directions

From the center of Chicago, take I-55 South for a little more than 13.5 miles until you get to Exit 279A-B, US-12 towards La Grange Road. Take US-12 East on the left side of the ramp and follow that for another 2 miles. At this point, merge onto Archer Avenue. After another 2 miles, the ballroom will be on your right.

history

The ballroom was originally created in 1921 and named Oh Henry Park. Throughout the 1920s, it was a popular destination for an evening out dancing. In 1930, disaster struck, as the ballroom caught fire and burned to the ground. No one was killed in the fire, but the fire threatened to end the year's business for the ballroom and ruin the owners. In an attempt to save the business, the owners hired hundreds of carpenters to build an outdoor dance floor where the site of the original ballroom had once been. Not only was the outside dance floor completed in time to bring in more business for the year, but it brought in more customers than it ever had before, due to the romantic notion of dancing under the stars.

Four years later, a young woman named Mary Bregovy was dancing at the ballroom with her boyfriend. The couple got into a terrible fight and, despite the frigid winter temperatures, Mary stormed out of the ballroom and began the long walk home down Archer Avenue. Soon after leaving the ballroom, a driver speeding down Archer Avenue struck her. She died that night from her injuries and the freezing temperatures. Her parents had her buried at Resurrection Cemetery down Archer Avenue, clothed in the same white dancing dress she wore on that fateful night. Today, many know her as Resurrection Mary.

ghost story

Resurrection Mary is a prolific ghost who haunts the path down Archer Avenue to Resurrection Cemetery (see Resurrection Cemetery and Archer Avenue chapters). She has also been known to haunt the Willowbrook Ballroom, where her last night as a mortal began. Resurrection Mary has been said to appear in the ballroom, and she will even begin to dance with some patrons before mysteriously disappearing into thin air. She is always seen wearing the same white dress and matching dancing shoes that she wore on her final night.

visiting

In order to enter the ballroom itself, you must enter during normal business hours. These hours change frequently from night to night, relative to different events held on different nights of the week. In order to determine the best time to go dancing with Resurrection Mary, one should visit the Willowbrook Ballroom website, willowbrook ballroom.com.

SECTION III
roads and bridges

AMERICAN AIRLINES FLIGHT 191 DISASTER SITE

351 West Touhy Avenue, Des Plaines, Illinois 60018

directions

From the center of Chicago, take I-90 West for a little more than 16.5 miles to the IL-72/Lee Street exit. Turn right onto Lee Street and follow it for about 2 miles before you reach the intersection with Mount Prospect Road. Continue straight. The crash site is the field to your right. The debris field is extended to the trailer park on your right.

history

On May 25, 1979, at 3:02 p.m., American Airlines Flight 191 began takeoff from O'Hare Airport. As the plane began rolling down the runway and approaching takeoff speed, the engine on the left wing detached and flipped over the wing. The engine tore off part of the wing and landed heavily on the runway. The flight crew, unable to see the engine from the cockpit, thought that the engine had simply failed.

Because they were already at speed, protocol with a failed engine demanded that they take off, turn around, and then land back at the airport.

The pilot's controls had failed, so the co-pilot took control and started the ascent. The damaged left wing failed, too, and the plane turned sharply to the right, almost inverting entirely. The plane dove from about 300 feet and the flight crew was unable to gain control of the aircraft. It crashed into a field just northwest of the intersection of Mount Prospect Road and Touhy Avenue. It was carrying enough fuel for a flight to Los Angeles, so it erupted into a huge ball of flame when it hit the ground. Flaming debris killed two people on the ground in a nearby hangar and other pieces of debris rained down onto the adjacent trailer park.

271 passengers and crew died in the crash, as well as two people on the ground, making it the deadliest aircraft accident and the second deadliest aircraft disaster besides 9/11 in American history.

Many airlines will no longer use the designation Flight 191 due to superstitions that the number is unlucky. Five Flight 191s have historically crashed, causing 398 fatalities.

ghost story

Soon after the crash, several people in the adjacent trailer park reported that there was a knock on their door. When they answered the door, they would find a person standing there who looked very confused. The person at the door would ask where they were, then would turn and walk away. As they began walking away, they vanished. Several people in the trailer park reported this happening.

The field itself is also reputed to be haunted. People have reported seeing a plane flying on its side crash into the field, and then leave no wreckage or indication that it had ever been there. Other witnesses have seen large groups of figures meandering aimlessly in the field. Upon investigation, the figures vanish.

visiting

The field itself and the trailer park are all private property, so you will be unable to actually walk out into the field or into the trailer park to look for the ghosts. This means that the only way to look for ghosts here would be to look for them while you are driving along the adjacent public road. There is a line of trees that will block your view for most of the stretch. This line of trees is much less obtrusive during fall and winter. During the summer and spring, there are still some breaks in the line of trees and a small spot where you can pull your car over and peer into the field from inside your car.

ARCHER AVENUE

Archer Avenue, Chicago, Illinois 60616

directions

Archer Avenue is a very long road that stretches southwest from Chinatown all the way to Lockport, Illinois. From the center of Chicago, simply take State Street to the south for about 1.5 miles. This will take you to Chinatown. Turn right onto Archer Avenue. Archer Avenue's name will change to Archer Road once you leave the city limits, but continue following Archer Road to stay on this haunted stretch of asphalt.

history

Archer Avenue itself was built along an old Native American trail. Legend has it that American Indians built this trail because of a mystical or magnetic force, which guided them along the south side of what would become Chicago.

Archer Avenue was named after the first commissioner of the Illinois and Michigan Canal, William Beatty Archer. Today, the road parallels the Illinois and Michigan Canal, as well as Alton Railroad. While the road was originally a major traffic artery, traffic along this stretch has decreased significantly since the construction of the Stevenson Expressway in October 1964.

Due to the haunted cemeteries along the road, as well as the plethora of ghost stories that people often tell about it, some say that the road is not only a paved road with lines, but a highway to another dimension.

ghost story

Some of the most famous stories about Archer Avenue are addressed in other chapters in this book. After all, this road is home to Resurrection Mary at the Willowbrook Ballroom and Resurrection Cemetery as well as St. James Sag Cemetery.

Beyond these staples of the area, the road is haunted by countless other spirits. Maple Lake often puts on a show for unsuspecting passersby. Ghost lights often take up residence in the Maple Lake area along Archer Avenue. Balls of inexplicable light dance across the lake and near the road. Often, these ghost lights appear for minutes at a time, allowing witnesses to watch in awe as they dance about for extended periods of time.

Beyond the most famous phantom hitchhiker of them all, Resurrection Mary (see Resurrection Cemetery chapter), many other phantom hitchhikers walk this haunted road. Many times the hitchhikers take the form of shadowy figures hitchhiking on the side of the road who suddenly vanish when you stop to pick them up. Other times, the hitchhikers appear normal when you pick them up, but, while you are driving them to their destination, you might look over to find an empty seat where they were sitting.

The road near St. James Sag Cemetery is haunted by a phantom hearse that is sometimes seen near the cemetery, only to disappear. Similarly, the road near Resurrection Cemetery is haunted by a phantom horse-drawn hearse that is said to vanish into a supernatural fog.

Beyond all of these, black mists and ghostly lights are seen all along this road, especially late at night.

visiting

This public road is open throughout the night. The best time to find its ghosts is very late. And the best area in which to find them is between Resurrection Cemetery and St. James Sag Cemetery. This is the most haunted and most remote section of the road. Be sure that if you are driving this area late at night, you keep a careful lookout for deer, as they are quite prevalent in the area.

AXEMAN'S BRIDGE
Old Post Road, Crete, Illinois 60417

directions

From the center of Chicago, take I-94 East for about 23 miles to Exit 74 A/B, the Bishop Ford Freeway toward Danville/Iowa/Wisconsin. Take this for a little more than 9 miles and then turn left onto East Richton Road. Follow Richton Road for 1 mile and then turn right onto Old Post Road. Follow Old Post Road for a little more than 0.5 mile until you reach a small creek called Plum Creek. You will find an old dilapidated bridge spanning the creek to your right. The bridge has now collapsed, but the rusted iron frame is still visible on the creek.

history

Whether the stories that circulate about the history of Axeman's Bridge are real or urban legends, they have gained a foothold in the culture and folklore of the area and must be mentioned when talking about the ghost stories here. There are two completely different stories about the axeman. Neither story has been verified historically.

The first story tells of a man who lived in the woods down a small trail from the collapsed bridge. The story has it that two young boys were dared by their friends to

run across the bridge and onto the man's property. The boys agreed and ran across the bridge. The man who lived there was not willing to let them do so, so he attacked and killed the boys with his axe.

The other story tells of a man who lived in the house down the trail from the bridge with his family. One day, the man took a walk with his mother-in-law and daughter out to the bridge. When they arrived at the bridge, the man went crazy and killed them both with an axe. After killing them, the man went back to the house, where he murdered the rest of his family. Leaving his family's bodies on the lawn, the man set fire to the house. Some say he died in the house, while others say that he watched the house burn until the police showed up. That version suggests that when the police showed up, the man fled to the bridge, where he was shot by police after taking a couple of them down with his axe.

ghost story

Sometimes those who drive by the area at night report seeing what looks like a house sitting in the woods, with soft yellow lights illuminating the windows. The house that once sat deep in these woods is no longer there. Are these lights an illusion, or are they the ghostly remnants of the house that once stood here? Others are said to hear a sharp pinging sound coming from the vicinity of the bridge. It sounds almost like a hammer hitting a metal plate—or perhaps like an axe hitting the iron bridge.

People report that their car will stall on the bridge on Old Post Road that crosses the creek adjacent to Axeman's Bridge. It is when the hapless passersby are helplessly stalled on the bridge that the screaming starts. Bloodcurdling screams echo through the woods and seem to be coming from the collapsed and rusted Axeman's Bridge. The screams sound like they are produced by different people—perhaps all of the victims of the supposed murdering spree that happened in the area.

visiting

Old Post Road is a public road that is open throughout the night. You can drive up and down the road to your heart's content, listening for the sounds of screams coming from the woods. Be careful if you choose to stop your car in the middle of the road. You don't want unsuspecting cars behind you to cause a collision. Your safest way to listen for the ghosts is to find a place to pull off the road and wait.

Access to the woods and to the bridge seems to be allowed from sunrise until sunset. At the time that this book was written, there were no posted signs prohibiting passersby from entering the woods. Feel free to park your car during daylight hours and walk back to the old bridge and down the trail to the site of the supposed murderer's house.

BLOOD'S POINT ROAD

Blood's Point Road, Cherry Valley, Illinois 61016

directions

This location is the farthest in the book from the center of Chicago and will likely take you a little more than 1 hour to get to. Start by taking I-90 West from the center of Chicago for about 71 miles to the Irene Road exit. Turn left onto Irene Road and follow this route for another 4 miles. At this point, you will hit Blood's Point Road. The road extends in both directions and the entirety of the road is reputed to be haunted. The railroad bridge will be on your right between Wheeler and Irene. The cemetery will be to your left, near where the road dead-ends at Pearl Street.

history

While the name of this road may sound ominous at first, it is actually named after a man called Arthur Blood, who was a prominent figure in Cherry Valley when it was first settled in the 1800s. A local legend tells of a woman named Beaula. Beaula carried with her a disgusting stench and was an incredibly ugly woman to look at. She was shunned by people from the area and some would even vomit at the smell and sight of her. According to the legend, Beaula had two children and decided one day to take them out to the railroad bridge on Blood's Point Road. One at a time, she hanged the children from the bridge, then hanged herself.

Much later, there was a tragedy involving a school bus on the same bridge. Somehow, on an icy winter day, the bus lost control and crashed over the side of the bridge. There was a moment when the bus teetered on the edge of the bridge, allowing everyone on board the grim opportunity of knowing their terrible fate. The bus fell to the ground and crashed, killing everyone aboard.

ghost story

The ghost of Beaula supposedly walks Blood's Point Road to this day. Sometimes, reports of her presence are nothing more than reports of a horrible smell of which a source cannot be found. Other times, people say they see red eyes glowing from the trees surrounding the road, or the visage of a hideous woman staring them down as they pass. Those who see Beaula's ghost report that she is so hideous that they vomit. A ghost cat—a black cat that supposedly once belonged to Beaula—is said to run in front of cars on the road, trying to make them crash. Some cars report hitting the cat but looking back to find no cat in the street. Beaula is most often seen in the area of Blood's Point Road between Wheeler and Irene, near the bridge where she supposedly hanged herself.

The horror of the day of the school bus crash is also seen and heard at night on Blood's Point Road. Witnesses report seeing school buses driving up and down the road in the middle of the night, which suddenly disappear. Witnesses who listen near the bridge say that they hear the sounds of screaming children.

Other phantom vehicles are spotted all up and down Blood's Point Road. People see tractor trailer trucks or vintage vehicles in the middle of the night; these are said to suddenly disappear, despite there being no place for them to have turned off the road. There is also a phantom police car, which will pull you over, then mysteriously vanish.

The cemetery is also reputed to be haunted by ghost lights. Rumor says that anyone who enters the cemetery will encounter bad luck.

visiting

The cemetery is closed to the public all day, daily. There is not a time when you can legally enter this cemetery, and it is closely monitored by a neighborhood watch program. Why? The cemetery's reputation as a haunted site often attracted thrill-seekers who turned to vandalism. If you do enter the cemetery, you will encounter bad luck, most likely in the form of prosecution for trespassing.

The road beside it, however, is public and is open throughout the night. Feel free to drive up and down it all night, attempting to experience some of the ghostly vehicles or sounds, or maybe be unfortunate enough to run into Beaula herself.

CAMP DOUGLAS

3306 South Cottage Grove Avenue, Chicago, Illinois 60616

directions

From the center of Chicago, take Lake Shore Drive to the south for a little more than 2.5 miles. Take the ramp to 31st Street and turn right onto 31st Street at the end of the ramp. This takes you along what was formerly the north side of the camp. Turn left onto South Rhodes Avenue and follow this down to 33rd Street. This takes you through what was previously the middle of the camp, down to the southern boundary of the camp. Turn left onto 33rd Street headed to Cottage Grove Avenue. Turning left onto Cottage Grove Avenue will take you to where the main entrance of the camp once was. The area is currently occupied by condominiums and a small park called Lake Meadows Park.

history

Camp Douglas was constructed as a Civil War camp in 1861. Originally built as a training ground for new Union recruits in the Civil War, the camp would more famously become a prison camp for Confederate soldiers. While the name Camp Douglas would always be its official name, many have come to know the site as the "Eighty Acres of Hell."

The camp first housed prisoners in February 1862 after the fall of Fort Donelson. Between 4,500 and 7,000 Confederate prisoners of war were sent to the camp. Only around 450 Union soldiers were there to guard them. Conditions for the prisoners at the camp deteriorated as more and more prisoners were interned here, raising mortality rates to as high as 23%. According to many accounts about the brutality of the camp, it was expected that almost one out of every four prisoners detained at the camp would die by war's end.

Most of these deaths were due to disease. Influenza, smallpox, and scurvy (due to insufficient vegetables in the prisoner's diets) killed hundreds of prisoners throughout the camp. Others died from the brutal Chicago winters due to insufficient clothing.

Some simply starved to death or died of thirst. As if these conditions were not enough, some prisoners were tortured to obtain valuable intel. Men were stripped naked and left in the freezing snow and ice for hours on end. Others were hung by their thumbs as a torture method to obtain enemy intelligence.

It is no wonder that those who were imprisoned here referred to this place as the "Eighty Acres of Hell."

ghost story

Today, the area is occupied by many condominiums and, according to some, the ghosts of those who lived and died here. People sometimes report the stench of dead bodies and decay in the streets, perhaps a vestige of the dead bodies that once piled up here. People also hear many ghostly things. Screams and crying can often be heard in this area. When witnesses search for the source of these sounds, no explanation is ever found. People also often report the sounds of men marching down the streets.

A large number of visual apparitions are also reported for this area. Most of the time, these apparitions take the form of men dressed in ragged clothing that vanish when approached. These men appear to people inside of the condominiums as well as to people walking or driving down the streets. The most often-seen apparition is that of a one-armed man in a Confederate uniform, who is seen outside of many of the condominiums within the area.

visiting

Of course, the condominiums are private property and are off limits to nonresidents looking for ghosts, but the surrounding area is open, and there are many sections of the old camp that you can explore throughout the night. Make sure that you exercise normal precautions when walking or driving through this neighborhood at night.

The best time to find ghosts in this area is after dark. Also, ghost activity tends to pick up whenever any kind of construction work is being done in the area. Sometimes, these construction projects dig up fresh graves and artifacts from the Camp Douglas days. When this occurs, the hauntings become much more frequent.

CLARENCE DARROW MEMORIAL BRIDGE

5700 South Lake Shore Drive, Chicago, Illinois 60637

directions

This location is about 15 minutes south of the middle of the city. Simply take Lake Shore Drive from the center of the city to the south for about 6.5 miles. There will be an entrance on your right called Science Drive. When Science Drive dead-ends, turn left toward the parking lot. This will bring you to the back of the Museum of Science and Industry. The Clarence Darrow Memorial Bridge is behind the museum and overlooks the Jackson Park Lagoon.

history

In late 1923, two men named Nathan Leopold and Richard Loeb decided that they would commit the perfect crime. They were considered geniuses, Leopold having an IQ of 210 and able to speak 27 languages fluently, and Loeb having been the youngest graduate ever of the University of Michigan. They decided that, due to their superior intellects, they could commit the "perfect murder."

They spent seven months meticulously planning it and set a date for May 21, 1924. The two men enticed the 14-year-old son of millionaire Jacob Franks, a boy named Robert "Bobby" Franks, to get into the passenger seat of their car. Leopold and Loeb then killed Bobby Franks, putting a sock into his mouth and hitting him over the head with a chisel. When they dumped the body in Indiana, Leopold dropped his eyeglasses at the scene. Only three people in the Chicago area had eyeglasses with the hinge mechanism on this particular pair. This led authorities to Leopold and Loeb.

The men went to trial for the murder, and lawyer, Clarence Darrow was hired to defend them, due to his anti-death penalty stance. Darrow succeeded in his plan. Instead, they were sentenced to life in prison. The trial was dubbed the "Trial of the Century" at the time.

Darrow would later become a defense lawyer in another "Trial of the Century," called the Scopes Monkey Trial, for which he defended a teacher who was arrested for teaching evolution at a school in Tennessee, where it was forbidden.

In 1938, Darrow died in his home on 60th Street, which overlooked Jackson Park. Darrow was cremated, and his ashes were scattered along the bridge and the lagoon. The bridge was named in his honor.

ghost story

Everything stayed quiet on the Clarence Darrow Memorial Bridge for the next 52 years. Then, in 1990, people began reporting strange things on the bridge. People said they would see the shadow of a man standing on the bridge. Sometimes, the man overlooks the lagoon. Other times, the man paces back and forth on the bridge for a little while, then walks farther into the park, where he vanishes into the darkness on the other side.

People who have seen the apparition have described him as appearing much the way Clarence Darrow looked in life. Because the figure is dark and shadowy, they are unable to describe any of the man's features. If the man is ever approached, he does not seem to notice that anyone else is there; it's as if he is in a completely different world. Eventually, he walks farther into the park and vanishes, or slowly fades away on the bridge, leaving onlookers wondering if he was ever really there, or if their eyes had been playing tricks on them.

visiting

The park is open until 11 p.m. daily. Because the ghost only seems to appear after dark, this 11 p.m. closing time does allow time to visit the site after dark has fallen. There is parking right next to the bridge and, if you go later at night, you will find it very empty. This emptiness is perfect for looking for this ghost.

CUBA ROAD

West Cuba Road, Barrington, Illinois 60010

directions

From the center of Chicago, take I-90 West for 26.5 miles to the Roselle Road exit. Follow North Roselle Road for about 4 miles, then turn right onto Baldwin Road. Turn left onto West Northwest Highway/US-14 West and follow that route for a little more than 6.5 miles before turning right onto Cuba Road. The haunted stretch of road begins at the intersection with Flynn Creek Drive and extends past White Cemetery

history

During Prohibition, gangsters from Chicago often vacationed in the area of Lake Zurich and Barrington along Cuba Road. They came here to fish or relax, far away from the stressful environment they had created in Chicago. But whenever they came into town, they would still manage to stir up trouble. There were rumors among locals of murders in the area, and there was a general sense of unease among them whenever the gangsters came into town.

Eventually, Prohibition ended, and the gangster scene in Chicago seemed to dissipate, especially for those residents of this area. Instead, Cuba Road became a place where teenagers raced muscle cars at high speeds in the middle of the night. In the 1970s, a car turning onto Flynn Creek Drive from Cuba Road crashed. All four students who were in the car were killed.

ghost story

Echoes of this road's tumultuous past seem to inhabit this stretch of road. The most often-reported paranormal activity along this stretch of Cuba Road involves ghost cars that will follow motorists before vanishing into thin air. People report being tailgated by circa-1960s muscle cars while driving down Cuba Road. As the scared drivers speed up to try to avoid them, the cars behind them suddenly vanish.

These cars are not the only ghosts along this stretch of road. People report seeing gangsters in old cars, as well as standing on the side of the road. When people see these gangsters, they usually only catch a glimpse of them through the rearview mirror of their car. This road is also infested with phantom hitchhikers. People encounter hitchhikers along the side of the road and sometimes stop to pick them up. As they are driving them to where they want to go, they glance over to where the hitchhiker was sitting, only to find the seat empty.

Orbs of light and shadows are also seen crossing the street near White Cemetery (See White Cemetery chapter).

visiting

This is a good place to look for ghosts. The road is open throughout the night, so you can spend as much time as you like driving up and down it looking for ghosts. The ghosts here are also seen quite often, so you may actually encounter something unexplainable if you drive this road at night.

DEATH CORNER IN LITTLE HELL

Oak Street and Cleveland Street, Chicago, Illinois 60610

directions

From the center of Chicago, take LaSalle Street to the north for a little more than 1 mile to West Oak Street. Turn left onto Oak Street and follow it for about 0.5 mile to the intersection with Cleveland Street. This intersection is known as Death Corner and consists mostly of empty lots.

history

Before the famous gang wars and bootlegging operations of Prohibition, an infamous Italian gang known as the Black Hand dominated the Chicagoland crimescape. From 1880 until the start of Prohibition in the 1920s, the Black Hand ruled parts of the city with intimidation. Perhaps the most lawless section of the city at this time was the area between LaSalle Street, Division Street, and the Chicago River. Many in the city knew this area as Little Hell. Arrests were common. Prostitution, robbery, and murder were exceptionally common, especially from 1900 until 1920.

The Black Hand often practiced extortion. Its members would prey upon successful business owners in Little Hell by sending letters demanding money for the privilege of operating in their territory. If any of these businesses did not pay, the owner would almost certainly end up dead.

The Black Hand employed many assassins to carry out the killings of those who refused to pay. The most famous of these assassins was known as the Shotgun Man, who is said to have committed at least 15 murders, including four that occurred during an exceptionally bloody three-day killing spree. These assassins often dumped the bodies of their victims in a place that became known as Death Corner, located on the corner of Oak Street and Milton Street (today Cleveland Street). The identity of the Shotgun Man was never discovered, and he ceased his attacks at the start of Prohibition around 1920, either having retired or having become a victim himself of the violence that gripped the city.

ghost story

Those who visit Death Corner in the current day report that there is something uncomfortable in the atmosphere that makes it unpleasant to be there. The air seems thicker than normal, and many state that they find it difficult to breathe. There is nothing physically different about the air, and yet, there is some kind of intangible force that creates a sense of discomfort in its visitors.

Beyond this strange feeling, people often see apparitions. Most of these are strange shadowy figures that move across the corner. Witnesses see these shadows out of the corners of their eyes, but when they turn to face the figure, they discover that it has vanished. Others have seen apparitions of people dressed in period clothing from the late 1800s or early 1900s.

visiting

While Little Hell is not quite as dangerous as it was in the early 20th century, it still is not the safest neighborhood in the Chicagoland area. If you do go to this corner late at night, be very careful that you do not put yourself in danger. While nighttime investigations may yield more sightings of shadows and apparitions, it is also much more dangerous than visiting during the day.

EASTLAND DISASTER SITE

Between Clark Street and LaSalle Street Bridges
on Chicago River, Chicago, Illinois 60601

directions

The site of the Eastland Disaster sits on the Chicago River between the Clark Street
and LaSalle Street bridges. From the center of downtown, simply take Clark Street or
LaSalle Street to the river.

history

Believe it or not, one of the worst maritime disasters in American history occurred in
the middle of downtown Chicago.

July 24, 1915, was a huge day for employees of the Western Electric Manufacturing
Company. The company was funding a large picnic for thousands of its employees up
in Michigan City. The employees were to be shuttled to the picnic on three large ships,
one of which was the *Eastland*. Since the sinking of the *Titanic* three years earlier, new
regulations were in place mandating that lifeboats be available for everyone on board.
Ironically, it would be the addition of these lifeboats that would doom the ill-fated ship.

It was already known that the *Eastland* was top-heavy and unstable. The added lifeboats and influx of passengers added to this instability. As passengers began boarding the ship, it began to tilt toward the starboard side at the dock. The crew filled ballast tanks on the port side of the ship to even out its weight. As the final passengers were boarding, more people walked to the port side of the ship. As additional people moved to the port, the ship began to tilt. Panicked passengers in the interior of the ship began to run to the deck. This was the last straw. As the majority of the passengers pushed their way to the deck of the already top-heavy ship, the ship lunged violently to its side and into the 20-foot-deep Chicago River.

Hundreds of people fell into the river from the deck of the ship and were pulled under by their heavy dresses and suits. Many did not know how to swim. Hundreds more were trapped below deck as the water rushed into the hull. Despite rescue efforts from the thousands of spectators, 844 people died in the disaster. Many of them drowned in the shallow waters of the river while thousands watched helplessly.

ghost story

Echoes of the disaster can be seen and heard to this day. Witnesses who walk across the bridge sometimes peer into the river below and see pale faces looking up at them from the shallow waters. Other times, people actually hear sounds of the terrible disaster when crossing the bridges at Clark Street or LaSalle Street. People hear screams echoing through the urban canyon or hear the sounds of sobbing. When these sounds are investigated, no source is ever found.

visiting

The bridges are open to foot traffic at all times of the day or night. The ghostly sounds and ghostly faces are seen and heard at all times of day and night. Your best chance of experiencing the ghosts here, though, is to go to one of the two bridges at 7:28 a.m. This is the time that the ship fell onto its port side.

FOX RIVER GROVE SCHOOL BUS ACCIDENT SITE

Algonquin Road and Route 14 NW,
Fox River Grove, Illinois 60021

directions

From the center of Chicago, take I-90 West for about 26.5 miles to the Roselle Road exit. Keep right on the ramp towards Palatine/Little City and then merge onto North Roselle Road. After about 4 miles, turn right onto Baldwin Road and then left onto US-14 West. Follow US-14 West for a little more than 9 miles to the intersection with Algonquin Road. Turn left onto Algonquin Road. The accident site is at the railroad tracks.

history

On October 25, 1995, a school bus being driven by a substitute driver stopped on Algonquin Road at the traffic light at Route 14. The bus was unable to completely clear the railroad tracks, so part of the back of the bus extended out onto them. Suddenly, a Metra commuter train bound for Chicago came barreling down the tracks. Not realizing that the back of the bus was still on the tracks, the school bus did not move in time. The train hit the back of the full school bus and broke it in half, knocking the back half of the bus into the intersection.

A police station was located directly across the street from the accident, and its response was instantaneous. For many of the children in the bus, though, it was too late. Five children were killed instantly in the accident, and two more died from their injuries. More than 20 additional students in the bus were seriously injured, though they did survive in the end.

ghost story

There are two facets of the ghost story told about this intersection. The first seems to be a replay of the accident itself. People report hearing screams and crying when they are near the accident site. Others say that they hear moans of pain. Still others hear voices crying out to move or to hurry. People who experience these replays of the accident also report feeling overwhelming sadness and a sense of loss. Many of the people who experience this do not even know about the bus accident that happened here.

The other facet of the ghost story seems more like an urban myth than the former. The story suggests that if you stop your car on the train tracks and put baby powder on the back bumper, your car will mysteriously begin to move by itself off of the train tracks. When you go to look at the bumper, you will see children's handprints in the baby powder.

visiting

Do not try the baby powder thing. This is likely an urban myth that seems to occur at pretty much every school bus accident site in the country. While it may be fun to try from time to time, these train tracks are still active, and it is incredibly dangerous to stop your car on the tracks and put it in neutral. There is also a police station almost directly across the street from the site. It's not a risk worth taking.

This doesn't mean that you cannot find any ghosts here. As long as you don't stop on the tracks, you can drive nearby and listen for the replay of the terrible accident that occurred. The area is located on public roads, so you can visit any time of the day or night.

FRANK "THE ENFORCER" NITTI'S SUICIDE SITE

7301 West 25th Street, North Riverside, Illinois 60546

directions

From the center of Chicago, take I-290 West for a little more than 8 miles to Exit 21B, the Harlem Avenue exit. Turn left onto Harlem Avenue and follow the road for a little more than 2 miles until you reach West 26th Street. Turn right onto West 26th Street and follow it to the first road on your right, which is called Veterans Drive. Follow Veterans Drive across the tracks and take your first right. This will take you past a water tower. The site is about 50 yards past the water tower. There is parking in a strip mall to your right.

history

Frank Nitti moved to Chicago and became one of Al Capone's most trusted lieutenants. He spent the early part of his Chicago career bootlegging and, when Al Capone went to jail for 11 years for tax evasion, Nitti was established as one of the leaders of Capone's outfit.

In 1943, Chicago crime bosses began to be indicted for extorting money from those in Hollywood. During a meeting, it was decided that Nitti should take the fall because the extortion was his idea and the informant was someone he had vouched for.

The day before the grand jury was meeting to discuss his case, Nitti told his wife that he was going for a walk. He left his house on Selborne Road and walked north toward the train tracks. He ended up in a train yard just north of 26th Street. By this time, he was drunk.

Nitti stood on the train tracks as a train began bearing down on him. Two employees at the train yard saw him and yelled warnings, and, at the last second, Nitti jumped out of the way of the train. Almost immediately, Nitti put a gun to his head and pulled the trigger. In a final second of indecision, his aim faltered and the bullet instead went through his hat. Still determined to kill himself, he aimed the gun at his head again and fired. Again, he missed, shooting another hole into his hat.

He succeeded in his third attempt to shoot himself.

ghost story

The ghost of Frank Nitti haunts the railroad tracks where he died, which now sit behind 26th Street near a strip mall just past a water tower. At night, when it is calm and quiet, people sometimes see a man walking alone along the tracks. The man is said to walk to the exact spot where Nitti died and will stagger before falling to the ground. The figure then disappears into nothingness.

visiting

Because it is located just off a public road, this area is open to the public at any time of the day or night. Do not walk out to the tracks. This is a dangerous move, as the tracks are still actively used. The best time to look for the ghost of Frank Nitti is at night, when it is quiet and there are fewer cars or people in the area.

GERMAN CHURCH ROAD

German Church Road, Willow Springs, Illinois 60480

directions

From the center of Chicago, take I-90/I-94 East for about 1.5 miles to Exit 53, I-55 South. Follow I-55 South for a little more than 16.5 miles to Exit 276A, South County Line Road. Follow South County Line Road for a little more than 1 mile, then turn left onto German Church Road. The haunted section of road is near the intersection of County Line Road and German Church Road.

history

On December 28, 1956, two young sisters named Barbara and Patricia Grimes left their home at around 7 p.m. to attend a movie at the local theater. They were never seen alive again. When their mother first reported them missing that night, the incident turned into a media sensation. At first, everyone thought that they had simply run away. Police officers scoured the adjacent forest. Thousands of flyers were circulated in the area. The girls had supposedly gone to see the Elvis film *Love Me Tender* that night. After their disappearance, the story spread so extensively that Elvis Presley himself asked the girls to return home.

Three weeks later, a man driving east down German Church Road saw two figures lying on the shoulder that he initially thought were mannequins. Further investigation proved otherwise. Lying on the side of the road were the bodies of Barbara and Patricia Grimes. They were completely naked and had frozen to death. Despite the long police investigation that followed, their killers were never found.

ghost story

The area where the bodies were discovered on German Church Road is haunted by a ghost car. Witnesses report hearing a car stop on the side of the road near where the bodies were discovered. They hear something that sounds like two heavy objects hitting the ground on the shoulder of the road. Then they hear a car quickly pull away. When witnesses hear these sounds, there is never a car visible on the road. Only the darkness of the night plays host to these creepy sounds.

visiting

German Church Road is open throughout the night. You can drive up and down the road to your heart's content or even pull over to the side of the road in an area that is safe to listen for the ghostly sounds. Turn east onto German Church Road from County Line Road, and you'll reach the spot where the ghost sounds are most often heard—near the intersection before you reach the adjacent subdivisions.

MUNGER ROAD TRAIN TRACKS

7N096 Munger Road, Bartlett, Illinois 60103

directions

From the center of Chicago, take I-290 West for about 22.5 miles to Exit 7, I-355 South. Follow I-355 for about 2 miles before taking the Army Trail Road exit. Keep right to merge onto Army Trail Road and follow it for about 9 miles before turning right onto Sutton Road. Follow Sutton for about 2 miles and then turn left onto West Stearns Road. Less than 1 mile later, turn left onto Munger Road. Follow Munger until you reach the train tracks.

history

There are many stories about people dying along the railroad tracks by Munger Road. While some of the stories have historic evidence to back them up, others are more likely urban myths that have been spread by the locals. Perhaps the most famous story involves a bus full of schoolchildren that was driving down Munger Road when it suddenly stalled out (other reports say it ran out of gas) on the train tracks. Before anyone could escape, a train crashed into the bus, killing all of the children inside. Another story reports that a man lived in a small shack that was situated near the train tracks. One day, a passing train suddenly derailed and barreled through the small building, killing the man who lived there. We were unable to uncover any historical evidence about these events occurring. Perhaps these stories are nothing more than urban myths that match the ghost stories. Since the road and tracks have been around since the late 1800s, it is highly likely that children have been killed by passing trains on this site.

There are, in fact, some documented cases of people dying along the train tracks by Munger Road. In 2000, a 31-year-old man was murdered in the adjacent forest preserve abutting the train tracks near Munger Road. He was beaten to death with a blunt object. Another murder involved a 21-year-old woman who was raped and murdered near the tracks in 1982.

ghost story

While much of the dark past of the area may include urban myths and events lost to history, enough ghostly happenings occur on Munger Road near the train tracks that a movie has been made about the ghosts who haunt it. The most popular story requires that you put baby powder on the back bumper of your car, stop the car near the train tracks, and put your car in neutral. The story suggests that the car will start to move toward the tracks. Further, if you get out and look at the bumper, you will see children's handprints in the baby powder. Sometimes, a ghost train will pass along the tracks as this is occurring. It is rare that anyone sees this ghost train, but people have reported feeling the breeze of a passing train and even hearing it passing.

Other stories about the area involve ghostly screams coming from the woods that surround the tracks at Munger Road. Others say that they see an older man who walks into the road to confront passing motorists in the middle of the night. The man eventually disappears.

visiting

Munger Road is a public road, so it is open throughout the night. That being said, it is important to be careful when visiting the area. The train tracks are still active. Do not, under any circumstances, stop your vehicle on the tracks in the middle of the night. Also, be cautious of other traffic on the road, especially if you are stopping in the middle of the road at the train tracks.

RANDALL ROAD AND STATE ROUTE 72 INTERSECTION

Intersection of Randall Road and Illinois Route 72,
West Dundee, Illinois 60118

directions

From the center of Chicago, take I-90 West for almost 40 miles to the Randall Road exit. Turn right off the exit to Randall Road and follow it for about 1.5 miles. This will take you to the haunted intersection of Randall Road and Route 72.

history

For quite some time, Randall Road has been considered one of the most dangerous roads in the state of Illinois. The road is long and straight, but it is dotted by subdivisions and retail establishments. The straightness of the road encourages many motorists to drive far too fast. Cars pulling out of side roads and businesses often do not realize that oncoming cars are coming so fast, and many traffic accidents have resulted. Because Randall Road is under the jurisdiction of Kane County and

State Route 72 is under the jurisdiction of the Illinois DOT, attempts to make the intersection safer have been delayed by arguments as to who will pay the bill for the improvements. Some changes were made to the intersection in 2008 in an attempt to lower the number of accidents, but the accident rate only rose higher.

In 2009, a nun was driving into the intersection and ran a red light, slamming into a vehicle containing four teenagers as a result. A 16-year-old boy in the car was killed in the accident.

ghost story

From time to time, people driving through the intersection at night report seeing a terrible accident unfold in front of them. Cars collide. Grinding metal and squealing tires are heard. Cars flip and come to rest within the intersection. The concerned, uninvolved motorist who witnesses the accident is said to pull his or her car over and approach the accident to help those involved. As the witness approaches the carnage, the entire accident scene is reported to suddenly vanish. Within an instant, there is no sign that an accident ever occurred.

While a phantom accident scene such as this can be disconcerting, some much more dangerous paranormal activity also occurs here. Some say that this paranormal activity is revenge enacted by the ghosts of those who have died on site, carried out against those who have done relatively nothing to make the intersection safer. People driving near the intersection are said to suddenly become groggy or incredibly tired as they approach. Until they reach the intersection, these drowsy individuals are said to feel no sense of fatigue. Perhaps this strange sense of grogginess has led to the recent increase in traffic accidents in the intersection.

visiting

This public intersection is open throughout the night. Much of the ghostly activity happens late at night, so this is the best time to approach the intersection. This being said, this intersection is still incredibly dangerous, so exercise extreme caution when approaching it.

SHOE FACTORY ROAD

Shoe Factory Road and West Higgins Road,
Barrington, Illinois 60010

directions

From the center of Chicago, take I-90 West for about 30 miles until you reach the Barrington Road exit. Take Barrington Road South on your left. Follow Barrington Road for less than 0.5 mile and then turn right onto West Higgins Road. Take your first left onto Shoe Factory Road. There will be a parking lot on your right, just past the intersection. Park here, then walk the bike trail. You will cross a small bridge over a creek and then come to a clearing in the woods. On your left will be the foundations of an old house, and to your right, the site where an old barn once stood.

history

Any dark things that happened occurred in the vicinity of the bike trail just off of Shoe Factory Road. A young girl was raped and murdered in the woods here. And an abandoned schoolhouse once sat along this road. It was broken into by vandals regularly until it was torn down in 2008.

On January 11, 1979, Marlene Manke, fiancée to Gary Teets, called Gary's brother, Earl Teets Jr., concerned about her fiancé and his parents. She had dinner plans with the family and arrived on time to their secluded farmhouse. But despite their plans, no one answered the door when she knocked.

Earl Jr. knew his parents well enough to know that something was wrong. He called the police, and two police officers went with Earl Jr. to the house. There was no answer when they knocked on the door. More concerned than ever, Earl Jr. put his shoulder to the door and broke into the house. Earl Jr. and the police walked into a slaughterhouse. One of the family's four guard dogs was shot to death. The other three dogs were locked up. Earl Jr.'s parents and brother were soon found as well— they were shot to death and left bleeding in the middle of the floor.

The case seemed easy enough. Due to the killer's apparent familiarity with the guard dog situation and the lack of struggle, the police assumed the killer to be someone who knew the family well. All that was left to do was find the evidence that had surely been left. Fate, it seems, had a different plan.

As the bodies were discovered, snow began to fall outside. Within the next four days, one of the largest blizzards to ever hit Chicago left more than 20 inches of snow on the ground. The secluded country roads were completely inaccessible. By the time the snow was cleared, a larger murder was entering the public consciousness. John Wayne Gacy's home was being searched, and body after body had been discovered in the basement. Many of the detectives who would otherwise have been investigating the Teets murder were investigating the Gacy murders. Finally, an arsonist snuck into the woods and burned the farmhouse to the ground, destroying any unfound evidence that was there. The Teets' killer was never found.

ghost story

Most of the ghost stories that surround Shoe Factory Road center around the foundation where the Teets' farmhouse once stood. In the woods surrounding the bike trail that leads to the house, people often hear the voices and the laughter of children. These sounds seem to follow these witnesses along the trail.

Upon the foundations of the farmhouse itself, people report hearing voices. These voices are different than those of the children who walk the path. These are adult voices. Some seem to be yelling. Some seem to be pleading. People who stand at the foundation of the house often feel overwhelming emotions of sadness and despair perhaps memories of the terrible event that occurred here in 1979.

visiting

Unfortunately, the bike trail passes through a Cook County Forest Preserve. As a rule, Cook County Forest Preserves are only open from sunrise until sunset. In order to look for ghosts along this haunted bike trail, you need to visit during daylight hours. Try to choose a time when it is not crowded, as you are much more likely to experience paranormal activity if you are alone.

SQUARE BARN ROAD

Square Barn Road, Algonquin, Illinois 60102

directions

From the center of Chicago, take I-90 West for about 40 miles to the Randall Road exit. Turn right onto Randall Road and follow it for 3 miles before turning left onto Huntley Road. Follow Huntley Road for a little more than 1 mile, where you will have to turn left again to stay on Huntley Road. Follow Huntley for another mile and Square Barn Road will be on your right. It stretches for a little more than 1.5 miles between Huntley Road and Algonquin Road.

history

The Algonquin area was once nothing more than a handful of farms and large expanses of farmland. Early legends about the area describe three adults, two men and a woman, who came across two small children in the area that is today Square Barn Road. The three adults surrounded the two young children and killed them one at a time. By the turn of the 20th century, those who lived in the area were well aware of the legend of the two defenseless children killed by the three adults.

Square Barn Road later become a hangout for a group of gypsies who would rob travelers who passed through the area at night.

In 1914, something strange started happening along Square Barn Road. The newspapers reported that locals were being chased by a "wild man" who wore no shirt or shoes and charged at anyone who passed through the area of Square Barn Road.

ghost story

The "wild man" is still seen along Square Barn Road from time to time. Those who see him report that he has a large, full beard and is wearing no shirt or shoes. He always approaches witnesses aggressively, often running at them full speed as if about to attack. The witnesses run away as quickly as they can, eventually turning around to find that the "wild man" is no longer behind them.

While the "wild man" is still seen from time to time, the most-often seen ghosts along Square Barn Road are those of the children who were reportedly surrounded and killed by angry farmers in the early days of Algonquin. People who drive down Square Barn Road at night report seeing two young children run out in front of the car, then disappear on the other side of the road. The children always appear to be frightened, as if they are running away from something or someone. As soon as the children cross the street, they vanish on the other side.

visiting

Square Barn Road is a public road that you can drive up and down all throughout the night. The ghost children are seen along all parts of Square Barn Road, but they are most often seen near the south end of the road near the Buena Vista Cemetery.

ST. VALENTINE'S DAY MASSACRE SITE

2122 North Clark Street, Chicago, Illinois 60614

directions

This site is just north of the center of Chicago. Take North LaSalle Street to the north from the center of the city for about 2 miles before turning left onto North Clark Street. After about 0.5 mile, you will pass Dickens Avenue to find the site of the St. Valentine's Day Massacre—a grassy area on your left that is sparsely populated by trees.

history

On February 14, 1929, seven associates of the North Side Gang, including retired gangster James Clark, met at a garage near the intersection of Clark and Dickens Streets. Gang leader Bugs Moran was supposed to meet them there for a business opportunity, but he fled when he noticed a police car in the area.

As the remaining seven members of the North Side Gang waited patiently inside the garage, two men dressed as police officers and two men dressed in plain clothes approached the garage as if carrying out a raid. They lined the North Side Gang members against the back wall of the garage. Suddenly, the four men opened fire on those standing against the wall. They unleashed hundreds of bullets from their Tommy guns into the men until they were all torn apart and laying on the floor. Two men, John May and James Clark, were then shot in their faces with a shotgun.

The police officers escorted the two men that they had walked in with at gunpoint back to their police car so as not to raise immediate suspicion. When the gruesome scene was discovered, only one of the seven men was still alive. Frank Gusenberg was discovered alive by police with 14 bullet wounds. The police asked him who had shot him. He answered, "Nobody shot me," and died three hours later. The general consensus about the massacre is that is was masterminded by Al Capone, leader of the rival South Side Gang. Capone himself was conveniently at a party out of state, where plenty of witnesses could report seeing him.

In 1967, the Clark Street Garage was torn down. The site was turned into a small landscaped area alongside a parking lot and a nursing home.

ghost story

Later in Al Capone's life, the mob boss took up residence in Chicago's Lexington Hotel. On many occasions during his stay at the Lexington, Capone's bodyguards would hear Capone begging someone to leave him alone. They would sometimes break into the room to see who was harassing their boss but would find Capone alone in the room. When they asked what had happened, Capone would tell them that he was being haunted by the ghost of James Clark, the retired gangster who died standing against the wall at the Clark Street Garage on Valentine's Day.

While a ghost or two may have followed Al Capone later in life, several other ghosts seem to have remained at the site where the massacre occurred. People often feel grief or anger when they are in the vicinity of the old Clark Street Garage site. More concretely, though, people actually see or hear ghosts in the area. The sound of distant Tommy gunfire is sometimes heard in the area, though no source for the sounds is ever discovered. Other times, people see men walking through the area wearing pinstriped suits. These apparitions are seen for only fleeting moments, then vanish into thin air.

visiting

This area is blocked off from Clark Street by a fence, but the area is accessible through a public alley that runs behind the buildings. The site is located beyond the street, so it does not really close. Today, the area is a grassy field with a handful of trees that sit between the street and the nursing home parking lot. You will be able to visit the location and look for ghosts during any time of the day or night. If you are there late at night, be sure to keep your own safety in mind. Also, exercise respect for those in the surrounding buildings, who are likely sleeping. There is not a time of day or night that the ghosts are more likely to appear, and while they have been seen or heard throughout the year, they are most prevalent around February 14.

SECTION IV

parks

CHANNING PARK AND SCHOOL

63 South Channing Street, Elgin, Illinois 60120

directions

From the center of Chicago, take I-90 West for about 36 miles to the IL-25 exit. Turn left onto Dundee Avenue and follow this for about 1 mile to Paige Avenue. Turn left onto Paige Avenue, then take your first right onto North Liberty Street. Follow Liberty Street for a little more than 1.5 miles, then turn right onto East Chicago Street. After about 0.25 mile, turn left onto Channing Street. The park and school will be on your left.

history

In 1845, the Elgin Burying Ground was established on the site where the school and park exist today. Eventually, the cemetery would change its name to the Channing Street Cemetery. By 1906, there were more than 3,500 graves within this site. 1906 was the date of its last recorded burial, and for the next four years, the cemetery became overgrown. Weeds and undergrowth overtook the cemetery. Headstones were lost in the undergrowth. Other headstones fell over and fractured. The cemetery was in terrible shape, and the city decided to create a park out of the cemetery as a solution.

They began the work to turn the cemetery into a park in 1915, but there were still many bodies in the cemetery at this time. Over the next 30 years, bodies were slowly relocated (see the Bluff City Cemetery chapter). By 1945, the cemetery was declared officially closed, but as the bulldozers began to clear the land for the park, they began exposing still more bodies. Caskets came out of the ground and cracked open, leaving body parts strewn across the landscape. Apparently all of the bodies had not been removed from the cemetery, leaving a grisly scene on the future parkland.

Eventually, the park and, later, the school would be completed on the site. Throughout the construction, many more bodies were discovered and moved to other cemeteries. Even recently, archaeologists have discovered 13 more graves in the area. Today, one grave remains in the southeast corner of the area. It is actually a marked grave containing the body of a man named William Hackman, who died in 1885.

Even to this day, people find chunks of coffin, pieces of tombstone, or even fragments of human bones in the park.

ghost story

The school itself is the most haunted section of this area. People in the school, especially the janitors who work there at night, report experiencing cold spots that they cannot explain, footsteps whose source is never determined, whispering all throughout the building, actual figures walking through the hallways, and objects moving of their own volition across the rooms and hallways. Some janitors are not brave enough to continue working here because of the frequent paranormal activity that they experience during the night.

While encounters within the school are more frequent, the park has much of the same ghostly activity. People hear footsteps behind them in the grass. People hear voices, see figures, and experience strange cold spots in the middle of the park.

visiting

The school is off limits to ghost hunters. The only people who may usually enter are students or employees of the school. However, members of the public are able to enter the park any time between sunrise and sunset. Although there are possibly more ghosts present at night, the grounds do close after dark, so in order to find the ghosts here, you will need to enter the grounds during daylight hours.

COVERED BRIDGE TRAILS

Walkup Road and Vermont Trail, Crystal Lake, Illinois 60012

directions

From the center of Chicago, take I-90 West for 26.5 miles to the Roselle Road exit. Keep right on the exit ramp towards Palatine/Little City and merge onto North Roselle Road. Follow this for 1 mile before turning left onto West Algonquin Road. Follow Algonquin Road for 13 miles before turning right onto Main Street. Follow Main Street for another 6 miles, then turn left onto Terra Cotta Avenue. Follow Terra Cotta Avenue for another 1.75 miles, then turn right onto Walkup Road. Follow Walkup for 1 more mile to the intersection with Vermont Trail. Turn left onto Vermont Trail. The haunted area is located at the covered bridge.

history

This area has always been rather remote and rural. Today, it is part of Chicago's suburbs, following the great suburban sprawl of the 1980s, but it is still a quiet place where not much happens. This is the way that the residents like it.

There is really no documented history that we were able to uncover about this location, but it is of course possible that there was a suicide near the location of this bridge, as suicides are not always documented.

ghost story

The water that runs beneath the bridge seems to have a life of its own. The water churns in very unusual ways from time to time. More amazingly, strange shapes sometimes form in the water, sometimes forming in three dimensions above the waterline itself. Balls of water sometimes lift out of the water and float above the surface for several moments before splashing back into the creek. Sometimes, lights lift out of the water and float around before diving back into the surface and extinguishing themselves.

The most famous ghost in the area also seems to be related to the strange behavior of the water. Sometimes, the water forms into the figure of a man. The man will be dressed in clothing from the 1950s and will often have his head in his hands. He appears to be weeping. Those who see his face report that he has a very depressed look in his eyes. Soon after he is seen, he splashes back into the water or simply vanishes into the air.

visiting

The bridge is on a public road that is open throughout the night. The biggest issue with looking for ghosts here is finding a place to park. There is no place on the side of the road that motorists are able to park. The easiest way to visit this site is to be dropped off. A bike trail runs along Walkup Road, so you can ride your bike up to the bridge. The bridge is open throughout the night, and there is actually a walkway for pedestrians that makes it easier to stand and look for strange happenings in the water. If you arrive during the day, you can walk north up the creek to look for the strange lights and noises that have been sighted in the water. The trails that run along the creek close at sunset, though, so after dark, you will have to stand on the bridge to look for ghosts.

DEAD MAN'S CREEK

1530 Brandywyn Lane, Buffalo Grove, Illinois 60089

directions

From the center of Chicago, take I-90 West for about 14.5 miles to I-294 North. Follow I-294 North for almost 12 miles to the Lake-Cook Road exit. Turn left onto Lake Cook Road and follow it for 4.5 miles before turning right onto McHenry Road. Follow McHenry for 1.5 miles, then turn right onto Deerfield Parkway. Take your first left onto Brandywyn Lane. After 0.5 mile, you will see a school on your left. Dead Man's Creek is behind the school, directly to the north.

history

Buffalo Grove was named for the large number of buffalo bones that were found in Buffalo Creek and the surrounding area. The area was originally mostly prairieland, but that has largely been replaced by modern development. Some of the only remaining prairieland in the area is a large grassy field behind Prairie Elementary School.

In the early days of Buffalo Grove, a man lived by himself in the woodsy prairie behind the school. There was a farmhouse and a large red barn on this site. One day, when the man was inside the barn, it caught fire. The flames spread quickly. After some time had passed and the flames leapt higher, the man turned his efforts from trying to extinguish the fire to escaping the burning barn. But by the time he tried to escape, it was too late. The fire had already barred all of his exits. He died within the building as it burned to the ground.

Nothing has been built in the area since the fire. Some say that people are afraid to go back there.

ghost story

Stories suggest that the man who burned to death near the creek haunts the area to this day. Perhaps the result of stories shared from student to student, people say that the man will try to kill anyone who is alone in the creek. They say that he wants others to suffer the same painful death that he did. When someone plays alone in the creek, the farmer is said to suddenly appear behind him or her. The intended victims, or at least the ones who tell the stories, always escape to recount their grisly tale. Some urban legends state that in order to summon the ghost of the farmer who died in the fire, you need to chant the words "dead man" twice.

Although the story regarding the ghost of the farmer seems like an urban legend used to scare local schoolchildren, perhaps discouraging them from venturing into the creek, ghost-hunting groups have also experienced strange phenomena in the area. Inexplicable feelings of discomfort seem to follow those who visit here, even in the middle of the day. Ghost investigation groups have also recorded strange electromagnetic readings here, which some people say are an indication that a spirit is attempting to manifest itself.

visiting

The school grounds and parking lot close well before evening, but the prairieland and creek behind the school are not on school grounds and do not close at sunset. That being said, it may be just as creepy to visit this haunted site during daylight hours because many of the reports here take place during the day. Be careful when walking out into the woodsy area surrounding the creek. Natural hazards are abundant, and these woods are much harder to navigate after dark. While the natural hazards are dangerous, if the stories about the ghost of the farmer are true, the supernatural hazards may be even more so.

EMMERICH PARK

151 Raupp Boulevard, Buffalo Grove, Illinois 60089

directions

From the center of Chicago, take I-90 West for about 14.5 miles to the I-294 exit. Follow I-294 North for about 11.5 miles to the Lake Cook Road exit. Turn left onto Lake Cook Road and follow it for about 5 miles before turning left onto Raupp Boulevard. The park will be on your left.

history

The park was created rather recently, having officially come into existence in 1992. During this relatively short history, no specific tragic events have been documented. There have been no disasters in the park. There is no documentation that anyone has actually died in the park or on the site where the park now sits.

There is a local story that may have something to do with the paranormal stories circulating around this park. Several decades ago, a local boy left his house for a bike ride and was never seen again.

ghost story

Some residents who live near the park have never actually been to it. They aren't sure why. They state that something intangible is somehow keeping them away, describing a strange feeling of discomfort whenever they consider going there.

The park is said to be haunted by a young boy. Children playing on the playground equipment often report strange happenings, including swings moving by themselves, even when there is no wind or anyone nearby. Children playing on the monkey bars report being pushed off by an unseen force. These children seem to be tormented by an unseen entity while they are trying to have fun.

Still, the most haunted place in the park is the bridge that crosses Buffalo Creek. Even the trail leading to the bridge from the southwest is haunted. People report feeling something tug on the bottom of their shirt and, upon turning around, they find no one there. People have often actually seen a young boy underneath the bridge with a bike. Sometimes, the boy is yelling, asking if anyone can hear him. When concerned witnesses try to help the boy, he vanishes.

visiting

Most of the paranormal activity in the park occurs during daylight hours. This is likely due to the fact that people are most often in the park during daylight hours. The park is open 6 a.m.–11 p.m., which means it is open for a couple of hours after darkness has fallen. Your best chance to encounter this ghost is to approach the bridge over Buffalo Creek at a time when no one else is there.

FORT DEARBORN MASSACRE SITE

East 16th Street and South Prairie Avenue,
Chicago, Illinois 60616

directions

From the center of Chicago, take South State Street to the south for about 1.25 miles until you reach 16th Street. Turn left onto 16th Street and follow it to the dead end. There are a couple of haunted locations in this area related to the Fort Dearborn Massacre. The first is located near the dead end at 16th Street at Prairie Avenue; just enter the field on your left. Next, if you follow Prairie Avenue down to 18th Street and turn left, you will find another park on your left, following a bend in the road. This is called the Battle of Fort Dearborn Park, and it is the second haunted location in the area.

history

When the war of 1812 began and Fort Mackinac fell to the British, it was decided that the Chicago stronghold Fort Dearborn was no longer defendable. Orders were given to evacuate the fort. Sensing that the Potawatomi Indians would mistake the departing soldiers and civilians as an attack, the captain held a meeting with the Potawatomi to advise them of the forthcoming evacuations.

On August 15, 66 soldiers and 27 women-and-children civilians exited the fort. The group headed south along the prairie near Lake Michigan, separated from the beach by a large sand dune. As they reached the area where 16th Street and Prairie Avenue exist today, the Potawatomi suddenly attacked with a force of about 500, cresting the top of the sand dunes and descending upon the unsuspecting troops. The line almost immediately broke, and the American forces were split. A group of Potawatomi charged at the wagon carrying the women and the children. Those soldiers who could attempted to defend them, but most of the children and soldiers in the area were killed, and the women were taken hostage.

William Wells witnessed the massacre at the wagon and attempted to help. He was almost immediately surrounded by countless Potawatomi. However, he fought bravely and managed to kill many of the Potawatomi before finally being killed himself. The Potawatomi cut out his heart and ate it on the battlefield, in order to absorb his courage.

The Americans were finally forced to surrender after losing 38 soldiers, two women, and 12 of the children. The other 41 were taken as prisoners.

It wasn't until the early 1980s that the location of the battle was rediscovered. Construction workers in the area unearthed bones, originally thinking that they were cholera victims from the late 1800s. Upon further research, it was determined that the bodies were from the early 1800s and could only be the victims of the Fort Dearborn Massacre. It was only after the bodies were moved and reburied elsewhere that people began seeing strange things in the area.

ghost story

Both the field near 16th Street and The Battle of Fort Dearborn Park just off 18th Street are haunted. While typically, when you have a haunted location, there are a variety of haunts that occur on site, these locations only have one type of reported haunting. People report seeing apparitions in these two places.

The apparitions are always described the same way. People see transparent figures—dressed in either pioneer clothing or military uniforms—wandering around the fields. Often, these figures appear frightened and are said to be screaming. This screaming, however, makes no sound. The apparitions are only seen and are never heard. Eventually, they just fade away into nothingness.

visiting

The field off of 16th Street contains railroad tracks that are still in use. Therefore, the area is actually private property that is off limits. When apparitions are seen in this area, they are typically spied from the adjacent road, which is open throughout the night. You can drive up and down this street throughout the night trying to find these apparitions. The Battle of Fort Dearborn Park is open until 11 p.m. daily. This means that the park is open for a few hours after dark, allowing you to park your car and explore the darkness, hoping to catch sight of those who perished here in 1812.

THE GATE

31738 North River Road, Waukegan, Illinois 60048

directions

From the center of Chicago, take I-94 West for slightly more than 21 miles to Exit 29, US-41 North towards Waukegan. Follow US-41 North for another 13 miles, then turn left onto Buckley Road at State Route 137. After following 137 for about 3.5 miles, turn right onto North River Road. Follow the road until it curves sharply to the right at the horse stables. Just to the left of the stables is a trail that leads to the gate.

history

This abandoned gate often strikes fear into those who believe the stories that circulate about the gate and the area beyond it. There are many different stories about what the gate leads to and the horror that occurred beyond it.

The gate led to a couple of different places throughout its life. First, in 1925, an orphanage called the Katherine Dodridge Kreigh Budd Memorial Home for Children stood here. But the orphanage closed by the 1950s, becoming the St. Francis Boys' Camp.

So far, the information presented above is true and undisputed, but there are many different stories regarding what occurred on this site. All of the stories share the same gruesome ending. As the story goes, someone went on a killing spree at the orphanage. Some say that it was the principal of the school, who had gone crazy. Others say that an escaped lunatic from a nearby asylum was the perpetrator. Still others suggest that an employee at the orphanage committed the crime. Whoever it was, this person chopped off the heads of four sleeping girls, placing their heads on the posts of the gate.

When the murders had been discovered, the residents of Libertyville were appalled. They couldn't bear being known for the horror that had occurred there. Some of the stories suggest that the townspeople burned the orphanage to the ground as a result. They wanted to eradicate any trace of the crime that had occurred.

ghost story

Some stories suggest that once the orphanage was burned to the ground and the boys' camp was constructed, the campers began to report strange happenings. They were grabbed by unseen forces. They heard shrieks and screams piercing the night air. They saw shadows of children playing in the moonlight.

People who approach the gate today report having strange experiences as well. Those who drive by the gate at night and stop their cars sometimes have trouble starting theirs cars back up again. Others hear children's laughter coming from beyond the gate. This laughter usually turns to screaming. Shadows of children move through the woods beyond the gate.

The most popular story involves the gate itself. At night, most often during a full moon, you can see four heads impaled on four of the gateposts.

visiting

The area beyond the gate is parkland and is only open from sunrise to sunset. The gate itself is visible from the public road. While you cannot park there and get out of your car to listen for the ghosts, you are able to roll down your windows and listen for ghostly sounds as you drive by. You are also able to look for the impaled heads on the gate as you drive by.

Visiting during the day is much easier. You can park at the Independence Grove Forest Preserve. This costs $5 during the week and $10 on weekends, unless you are a Lake County resident. There is free parking at remote Milwaukee Avenue, but this will necessitate an extended hike.

JOLIETARSENAL

20953 West Hoff Road, Elwood, Illinois 60421

directions

From the center of Chicago, take I-55 South for about 52 miles to Exit 241 toward Wilmington. Turn left onto North River Road and follow that for another 4 miles to IL-53 North. Follow IL-53 North for about 3 miles. The Midewin National Tallgrass Prairie will be on your right and the Abraham Lincoln National Cemetery will be on your left. These were all part of the Joliet Arsenal grounds.

history

The Joliet Arsenal was an ammunition plant opened in 1940 as World War II raged in Europe. By 1942, the ammunition plant was in full swing and production was going 24 hours a day, seven days a week, to meet the demands of the war raging in both the Pacific and in Europe. On June 5, 1942, at 2:45 a.m., tragedy struck the plant violently. A static spark on an assembly line ignited the explosives. The building detonated.

The explosion was felt as far away as Waukegan, which was 60 miles north of the accident. Most of the people in the building were killed instantly. All told, 48 people were reported dead or missing by the time that the wreckage was cleared.

Eventually, the arsenal was used during both the Korean and Vietnam Wars. The plant ceased operations in the late 1970s, never to be used as an ammunition plant again. Today, the site has been redeveloped. It currently houses the Abraham Lincoln National Cemetery and Midewin National Tallgrass Prairie.

ghost story

To this day, people report seeing the workers who died in the 1942 explosion at the site of the accident. The workers appear to be going about their work, although the building and the machinery are no longer there.

IL-53, which runs through the site of the old facility, is haunted by a host of ghost cars. Cars are said to suddenly appear or disappear. Others may be visible but cannot be heard. Other cars may be heard but cannot be seen. People also hear footsteps near them when they are in the area, even though no one is there.

While some people attribute these strange goings-on to ghosts from the old ammunition plant, others attribute the paranormal happenings to more surreptitious things. They state that secret research likely occurred at these government plants and that the paranormal activity is a residual effect of their top-secret research.

visiting

Many of the original buildings here have been fenced off or demolished, but there are still several bunkers open to the public. The Lincoln Cemetery and prairieland are also open to the public. Their visitation hours are listed as one hour before sunrise to one hour after sunset. Do not enter the grounds after these posted hours.

The road that passes through the area, IL-53, is a public road that is open throughout the night. Feel free to drive up and down this road all night long looking for ghost cars.

MAGIC HEDGE

West Montrose Harbor Drive, Chicago, Illinois 60640

directions

From the center of Chicago, take North Lake Shore Drive for about 4.5 miles until you get to the Montrose Avenue ramp. Turn right onto Montrose Avenue and follow it until you reach West Montrose Harbor Drive. Turn right onto Montrose Harbor Drive. The Magic Hedge will be on your left. There will be parking past the Magic Hedge on your right near the harbor.

history

In the 1950s and 1960s, Montrose harbor was used as a missile base to protect the city of Chicago from Soviet bombers in case there was ever an attack. The two most notable characters from the time were named Pique Nerjee and Hernando Rodrickkez. While these two were essentially friends, they constantly argued about everything and would often get into fights at the base. One Halloween, the pair got into a heated argument that ended with Rodrickkez screaming, "I'm going to kill you." Nerjee is said to have stormed off to the barracks, while Rodrickkez attended a Halloween party on the base.

During the party, a huge bang was heard throughout the base that seemed to originate at the barracks. Being a religious and superstitious man, Rodrickkez thought that he had somehow wished Nerjee dead. In terror, Rodrickkez raced toward the barracks screaming, "Pique, Pique! Please, Pique!" When they found Nerjee in his bunk, he was dead. There was no apparent cause of death. Not even the coroner was able to determine what had killed him.

Rodrickkez, somehow mentally broken by what had happened, ran out of the barracks and into the night. Despite exhaustive searches, he was never found again. It was assumed he killed himself by drowning in the freezing waters of the lake.

Eventually, the missile base was torn down. All that is left are the hedges that once surrounded the missiles.

ghost story

It seems that Nerjee and Rodrickkez continue to haunt the area where they became friends and died. Often, people report seeing two shadowy figures who look and sound as if they are arguing. These shadows are seen in the vicinity of the hedge. When witnesses approach the figures, the apparitions vanish without a trace.

Beyond seeing the figures, people also sometimes hear the voice of Rodrickkez from beyond the grave. Rodrickkez's chilling last words before running off into the night are said to echo near the hedge. People hear a disembodied voice say, "Pique, Pique! Please, Pique!" The source of the voice is never found.

Even if these strange things don't occur, people still report feelings of extreme discomfort from time to time in the vicinity of the hedge. Some have even reported being attacked by vampire bats when in the area after dark.

visiting

Today, the Magic Hedge is a bird sanctuary. It is a noted bird-watching location in the Chicago area, and most everyone that you see in the area will come armed with cameras and binoculars. When entering the area, be sure to stay on the marked trails because the surrounding vegetation and wildlife is rare and protected. You will only be able to enter the area during daylight hours. It is closed from sunset until sunrise.

MAPLE LAKE

95th Street and Wolf Road, Willow Springs, Illinois 60480

directions

From the center of Chicago, take I-55 South for a little more than 13.5 miles to Exit 279A, the La Grange Road exit. Merge onto US-20 East and follow that route for almost 2 miles before merging onto Archer Avenue. Follow Archer Avenue for a little more than 3 miles, then turn left onto 95th Street. Maple Lake will be on your right, just past the intersection with Wolf Road.

history

Maple Lake is a manmade lake. When it was first constructed, it was used by locals recreationally. People fished and picnicked during the day. Others walked along the lakeshores or swam in its waters. The area was also once used by teenagers as a sort of "lovers' lane," a place for couples to escape to engage in amorous activities.

    In the early 1990s, the reputation of this lake began to falter, as several young women ended up dead along its shores. It seemed that someone was killing young women and dumping their bodies into the lake. The murderer—or murderers—of these young women was never found.

While we were unable to uncover any historical evidence to back it up, there is another story that circulates about this area. This story predates the lake, at a time when the area was all farmland. As legend has it, a farmer who was working the fields had a terrible accident with a heavy piece of farming machinery. He fell into some blades and was decapitated.

ghost story

The story has it that the decapitated farmer searches the area with a reddish lantern, looking for his lost head. Maple Lake is home to Chicagoland's most famous ghost light. From the lakeshore near 95th Street, people report seeing a reddish-yellow light move across the water near the opposite shore, then disappear into the woods beyond the lake.

The light has been seen by countless people. Many of them have heard about the light and do not expect to actually see it when they go. When they do see it, they do whatever they can to investigate the light's source. They are never able to find any explanation. Some theories suggest that pranksters are running through the forest with flares, but those who have seen the light discount this as a possible explanation due to the light's original position over the water.

Whether the ghost light is actually the ghost of the farmer who lost his head, one of the many women who were found along the lake's shores, a UFO, or some sort of strange atmospheric phenomenon, it is definitely one of the most often-seen and famous paranormal occurrences in the Midwest.

visiting

The ghost light is seen exclusively at night. This causes some potential problems for seeing the ghost light because the forest preserve itself closes after nightfall. 95th Street runs directly adjacent to the lakeshore, though, and is a public road open throughout the night. From 95th Street, you will be able to peer across the lake to the point where the ghost light is always seen. Be very careful when stopping your car along 95th Street in the middle of the night. The road is curvy and cars often travel up and down the road at high speeds. If possible, try to find a place to pull off the road to watch the lake for the ghost light.

RACEWAY WOODS

17 II-31, Dundee, Illinois 60118

directions

From the center of Chicago, take I-90 West for about 37.5 miles to State Route 31 North. Follow 31 North for a little more than 4 miles. There will be a parking area for Raceway Woods on your left. If you reach Gentle Breeze Terrace, you've gone too far.

history

While a forest preserve today, these woods were once home to the Meadowdale International Raceway. This automobile racetrack was built in 1958 in the suburbs of Chicago in order to entice development in the Carpentersville area. The track gained much popularity during its construction and leading up to the spectacular opening race on September 13, 1958.

Many accounts state that as many as 150,000 people arrived as spectators on the opening day of the racetrack. The racing began at a furious pace and cars began speeding around the track's many embankments and turns. Unfortunately, in a rush to prepare the track for the race, many shortcuts were used in engineering, and one of the drivers ended up flipping his Ferrari during a sharp turn known as Doane's Corner. The car did not have rollover bars, and the accident ended up snapping the driver's neck. The driver died on the way to the hospital.

Although this was the only fatality ever reported at the racetrack, the track retained its reputation as a killer track because of it.

The site was purchased by local park districts from 1994 through 2002 and is today a park known as Raceway Woods. Much of the original track is now trails featuring some of the original pavement from when it was one of the most popular tracks in the area.

ghost story

While the grandstands are gone and the track itself is hardly recognizable as the racing mecca that it once was, memories of its past still echo audibly through these woods. People often hear the sounds of the racetrack when walking through these woods along the trails that were once the track itself. Distant cheering—perhaps echoes of the opening-day crowd—have often been heard throughout the park. The sounds of racecars and revving engines have also been reported throughout these woods.

Perhaps the most haunted section of the park is the area that was once known as Doane's Corner, where the fatal accident occurred. Strange orbs of light are often seen in this area. Strange sounds that have no apparent source are also heard here.

visiting

The park is open from sunrise until sunset, so you will need to enter the park during these times if you want to walk the former raceway. Parking on both Route 31 and Huntley Road is met with trails to the path. Parking on Huntley Road is much closer to Doane's Corner, which is on the west side of the track.

ROBINSON WOODS FOREST PRESERVE

4850 East River Road, Chicago, Illinois 60656

directions

From the center of Chicago, take I-90 West for a little more than 12.5 miles to Exit 79B, the North Cumberland Avenue exit. Turn left onto Higgins Road and follow that for about 0.5 mile to East River Road. Turn left onto East River Road and follow it for approximately 1 mile to a small parking area on the right side of the road, located near a small burial ground in the woods. If you reach Lawrence Avenue, you've gone too far.

history

The Robinson Woods Forest Preserve was first owned by a man named Alexander Robinson. Robinson was a chief of the native Potawatomi, Ottawa, and Chippewa American Indian tribes, but only maybe a quarter of his ancestry was American Indian. After the Fort Dearborn Massacre, Robinson worked hard to aid the survivors. As a reward for this, he was granted the land along the Des Plaines River between Lawrence Avenue, where I-90 is today. The woods became known as Robinson Woods, and Robinson and his descendants lived here from 1829 to 1955.

Throughout the years that they lived there, many generations of Robinsons were buried on a family plot near River Road in the preserve. Because they lived without running water, those who lived in the house on the property had to walk down to the river to get water. When they needed to retrieve water at night, they were known to carry torches through the forest, down to the river, and back. In 1955, the house on the property burned to the ground. Although no one was killed in the fire, the fire marked the end of the Robinsons living on the land. That same year, just across Lawrence Avenue from Robinson Woods near the Des Plaines River, three bodies were found strangled to death in a ditch. The victims were 11, 13, and 14 years old. Their killer wasn't arrested until 1995.

One of Alexander Robinson's last descendants, Herbert Boettcher, had asked to be buried with his ancestors in the Forest Preserve. But when he died in 1973, the Illinois Forest Preserve District denied this burial petition due to sanitary reasons. That was when the hauntings began.

ghost story

While the last of Alexander Robinson's descendants have moved away from these woods, something still inhabits this site. The woods seem to be constantly teeming with activity that is at best unexplainable, and at worst terrifying. Tribal drumbeats sometimes echo from far out in the woods, a distant reminder of the American Indians who lived here before Alexander Robinson took over the woods.

The trail that starts at the left of the burial ground and leads off toward the river is where most of the paranormal activity takes place. People report seeing orbs of light that travel through the woods and then mysteriously vanish. At night, although the area is closed to visitors, people see what appear to be torches moving slowly down the trail toward the river. People who walk this trail, even in the dead of winter, are said to smell the overpowering aroma of lilacs.

Other entities besides these lights and smells also haunt the trail near the burial ground. Witnesses who walk down this trail sometimes see faces peering out at them from the forest, perhaps watching these trespassers invade their ancestral grounds.

visiting

There is a small parking area alongside East River Road near the Robinson burial ground. The trail that you must take to experience these ghosts is to the left of the headstone that marks the burial ground. Most of the paranormal activity is experienced during the day. The smell of lilacs can be encountered at any time of year, but it is considered more unusual during the winter when nothing can bloom in the forest.

Because the area closes at sunset, you must remain in the parking area or on the road to see the torches disappearing down the trail into the forest.

SUNRISE PARK

1200 South Appletree Lane, Bartlett, Illinois 60103

directions

From the center of Chicago, take I-290 West for about 22.5 miles to Exit 7, I-355 South. Follow I-355 for about 2 miles before taking the Army Trail Road exit. Keep right to merge onto Army Trail Road and follow it for a little more than 8.5 miles. Turn right onto Sutton Road and follow that for a little more than 1 mile. Turn right onto Struckman Boulevard, then 0.5 mile farther, turn right onto Appletree Lane. These roads take you through Sunrise Park.

history

Sunrise Park is one of the largest parks in Bartlett and currently houses a pond that Boy Scouts use for fishing, as well as a large disc golf course. The park is also used for cross county meets for the local high school. The park seems rather normal at first glance.

Much of Bartlett, including parts of this park, was formerly used by American Indians as burial grounds. Throughout the years, many of these burial sites were lost, and it is entirely possible that some Indian graves still lie beneath the dirt at this park.

There is also a bit of strange local lore involving a 40-year-old man who lived alone in a house by a school in the area. The story takes place in the early 1800s and often involves a small schoolhouse that stood near the corner of Route 59 and Smith Road. People often complained about screams coming from the man's house and from the surrounding woods. The parents who sent their children to this school became concerned about their children's safety and petitioned to have the man's house destroyed. As a result of their complaints, the house was destroyed and the parents no longer had anything to worry about. Or so they thought.

ghost story

According to local legends, the man died shortly after his house was destroyed. He credited his declining health to the loss of his house and blamed the complaining children for the destruction of his home. After he died, one by one, children began to disappear in the woods at Sunrise Park. People found small bones in the woods, perhaps the bones of the children. They always were surrounded by small piles of wood. According to these legends, children continued to disappear throughout the 1800s and up until the present day.

While the tale of the disappearing children is likely just an urban myth meant to scare and excite the locals, odd things do happen in this park. Many people report a strange and intangible feeling of discomfort when they walk through it. Others report that they find it hard to breathe while walking through the park at any time of day. Perhaps the most often-reported paranormal incidents in this park are its sounds. At night, people still hear screams coming from the woods. Apparently, destroying the man's house accomplished nothing.

visiting

The park is open from sunrise until sunset, so you may only enter the park during this designated time frame. The screams are almost exclusively reported at night. This is OK, though, because you do not have to be inside the park to hear the screams. These screams are often reported by those beyond the park grounds. Find a place nearby to park your car, roll down your windows, then listen for the ghostly screams to pierce the night.

TROUTPARK

Trout Park Boulevard and Sherwood Avenue,
Elgin, Illinois 60120

directions

From the center of Chicago, take I-90 West for about 36 miles to the IL-25 exit. Turn left onto Dundee Avenue, then take a right onto Trout Park Boulevard. The park will be on your right, and the entrance will be near the intersection with Sherwood Avenue.

history

There is something pleasant and peaceful about the atmosphere of this park. Beautiful cliffs and ravines house trickling streams and waterfalls. The wildlife and flora in the area are somewhat unique to the area. It was considered so beautiful that, in 1909, an amusement park was built on the site. There was a roller coaster, a spinning swing ride, and a famous carousel. Eventually, however, the bills outweighed the popularity of the amusement park and it was abandoned. No vestiges of it remain.

Even after the fall of the amusement park, the area still remained a popular destination due to its natural beauty. But there was soon a flipside to this coin. The tranquility of this place made it a magnet for a much darker type of person. People who were depressed and intent on ending their own lives flocked to the park. Many suicides occurred here, most of them by hanging or by gunshot.

ghost story

An aura of depression and perhaps the spirits of those who took their own lives have remained behind. Many visitors report feeling strange presences while in the park. They feel that they are being watched or that there is someone nearby, even when they are completely alone. Other times, people hear what sounds like sobbing or crying. Those who hear these sounds seem to sense it coming from all around them. They are unable to locate the source of the crying, despite sensing that the crying is coming from the very spot where they are standing.

Other witnesses to the paranormal report seeing orbs of light floating through the park. These balls of light float along only to disappear into the trees or simply fade into nothingness.

visiting

In order to experience any ghostly activity in this park, you will have to actually enter the park itself. The park is only open from sunrise until sunset. But those who have experienced ghostly activity here often report having experienced it during the day, when they are alone and in a remote section of the park.

WRIGLEY FIELD

1060 West Addison Street, Chicago, Illinois 60613

directions

From the center of Chicago, take I-90 West for 2.5 miles to Exit 48A, the Armitage Avenue exit. Turn sharply right onto West Armitage Avenue, then take your second left onto North Ashland Avenue. Follow Ashland for 2 miles before turning right onto West Addison Street. Wrigley Field will be on your left after a little more than 0.5 mile.

history

Slightly more than a month before being elected President of the United States, democrat Franklin Delano Roosevelt sat in the stands at Wrigley Field. It was game three of the 1932 World Series. It was the top of the fifth inning. After having fallen behind 3-0 in the first inning, the home team, the Chicago Cubs, had fought back to tie the game at 4. Charlie Root was on the mound as Yankees slugger Babe Ruth stepped up to the plate.

Ruth opted not to swing at the first pitch, and the ball caught the strike zone, smacking the catcher's mitt. The stadium erupted into applause and taunts extended from the Cubs' bench. The next two pitches missed the zone, then the fourth pitch again caught the zone, causing the stadium to erupt into cheers. The count was 2-2. Then, something unheard of happened. Only in baseball—where the rules never change, and a game played in 1932 could be the same game played today—could a story like this be passed down from generation to generation without becoming antiquated. As Root prepared to pitch, Ruth extended the index finger on his right hand and pointed toward center field. Root delivered. Ruth swung and connected. Few who were present that day or who heard about the hit would dispute that, as the ball sailed over the center field wall, it was the stuff of legend. Despite how audacious or pretentious calling his home run might have been, Babe Ruth is, and will always be, remembered for that incident.

The Cubs were swept in that series. And it wouldn't be the last World Series they would lose. As any Cubs fan knows, the team holds the record for the longest losing streak between world championship wins in the world of professional sports. They have not won a World Series since 1908. They have never won a World Series since they moved to Wrigley Field in 1916, two years after it was built. In Chicago, though, this doesn't matter. Once a Cubs fan, always a Cubs fan. Even though the Cubs haven't won the championship for more than 100 years, they will always have their fans. The fans are there through the good times and the bad, through the legendary moments and the quiet seasons that fade into history. They stand by their Cubs in the oldest stadium in the National League and the second-oldest stadium in professional baseball, Wrigley Field. Some of the greatest fans, such as announcer Harry Caray, songwriter Steve Goodman, and player-manager Charlie Grimm, have likely remained here after their deaths.

ghost story

Three famous ghosts are said to haunt Wrigley Field. The first is that of legendary announcer Harry Caray. The ghost of Harry Caray most famously haunts the press box and the adjacent bleachers at the stadium. Most people who experience Caray's ghost report an unexplainable feeling and a presence they cannot see. Others report strange mists that they attribute to Caray's ghost.

The next ghost is that of songwriter Steve Goodman, who not only wrote many songs about his beloved Cubs, but also had his ashes scattered at Wrigley Field when he died from leukemia in 1984, at the age of 36. People sometimes report seeing the ghost of Steve Goodman sitting in the seats behind home plate, watching the Cubs play on even after death.

The third ghost is Charlie Grimm, the manager who led the Cubs to the 1932 World Series. Security officers roaming the ballpark after dark have reported hearing the phone in the bullpen ring on its own accord. Guards have also reported hearing their names called by an unseen entity and have actually seen a figure resembling Grimm walking through the park or its hallways. They attribute the bullpen phone and the name-calling to Grimm because his ashes live on in this place. They are supposedly housed in a private box in left center field.

visiting

While the best time to visit a ballpark is always on game day, Wrigley Field also offers guided tours throughout baseball season, during which you can visit places that the public is not often able to go. Regardless of when you go, it is well worth a trip to this legendary site. Wherever you sit, you may experience the ghosts of any of the Cubs fans who have passed through this park over the last 100 years.

SECTION V

museums, theaters, hotels, and other buildings

ANTIOCH DOWNTOWN THEATER

378 Lake Street, Antioch, Illinois 60002

directions

From the center of Chicago, take I-94 West for about 48.5 miles to the IL-173/ Rosecrans Road exit. Turn left onto Rosecrans Road and follow it for about 7 miles before turning right onto Main Street. Follow Main Street for 0.5 mile before turning left onto Lake Street. The theater will be on your left near the intersection.

history

This building was originally a store called the Barney F. Nabor Store. In 1919, it was remodeled into the Majestic Theater, where stage plays were performed. The building was soon transformed into a movie theater and, by 1930, changed its name to the Antioch Downtown Theater. It has continued to operate as a movie theater since that time.

A popular story has it that a young, depressed woman once hanged herself from the balcony during a movie.

ghost story

Whether or not the story about the woman who hanged herself here is true, many employees and patrons have experienced strange happenings throughout the building. When the place is quiet, strange banging is said to come from within the building. Those brave enough to investigate the sounds are unable to locate the source. Footsteps follow people throughout the theater, even when there is no one there. People feel as if there is someone else with them in a room, even when they are alone.

More tangible things have happened here as well. People actually see figures that disappear suddenly. Other times, the flood lights in the auditorium turn on by themselves without anyone flipping the switch.

visiting

In order to enter this theater, you will have to purchase a ticket to a movie screening. The showtimes vary from week to week, but typically run noon–10 p.m. Arrive a little early to explore the auditorium in search of ghosts. Your best bet for finding something unusual would be to go to the theater when very few people are present. Because this is a movie theater, video cameras are prohibited within the building.

ARCADA THEATRE

105 East Main Street, St. Charles, Illinois 60174

directions

From the center of Chicago, take I-290 West for 16.5 miles to IL-64 West, Exit 13B. Follow IL-64 West for a little more than 20 miles. The theater will be on your left.

history

The theater presented a silent film at its grand opening on Labor Day 1926. Seemingly ignoring the fact that the town of St. Charles was populated by only around 5,000 people, the theater was built with more than 1,000 seats. As ambitious as it was to build such a large theater in such a small town, the theater sold out for months after the grand opening.

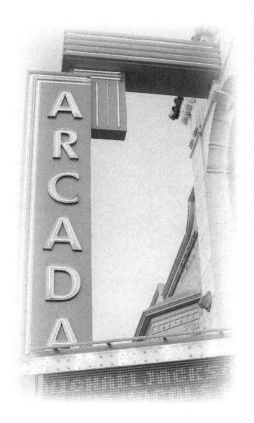

According to some, the basement and tunnels that run underneath the theater were originally used in the mid-19th century as a part of the Underground Railroad and a method of transporting escaped slaves to Canada. The tunnels were later used as a brothel and by bootleggers to transfer alcohol discreetly. Several murders were rumored to have taken place in these secret passages.

Several years after its opening, the theater phased out the silent films that had been so popular at its inception and began showing films with sound. These films were just as popular, and the theater has remained in almost constant operation since its opening in 1926, save for a few brief periods of renovation. Throughout these many years of operation, some of the biggest names in film watched movies within this very building. Stars such as Mickey Rooney, Jerry Lewis, Dionne Warwick, and Wayne Newton sat in these very seats.

ghost story

Film stars from the silent era of movies have supposedly taken up residence in this early mecca for silent films. Many of these film stars lost their jobs and their livelihoods when "talkies" became the staple of film. Legend has it that a few of them still hold grudges, and they haunt the theater as a result. People have seen apparitions of these silent film stars. Not surprisingly, these ghosts never talk.

Voices and sounds are often heard throughout the theater. The sounds are most prevalent in the balcony, where many people claim to hear voices and footsteps, even when the balcony is completely empty. Light fixtures swing back and forth, despite there being no breeze to rock them. Inexplicable spots of extreme cold and strange smells have been reported throughout the theater as well. Beyond this, shadowy figures and sounds are sometimes heard in the basement.

visiting

In order to enter the theater, you must buy a ticket to a movie and attend as a patron. Even if you do not encounter a ghost while watching the film, the ticket will be well worth the price to experience this piece of cinematic history.

BAYMONT INN AND SUITES

308 South Lincolnway, Aurora, Illinois 60542

directions

From the center of Chicago, take I-290 West for a little more than 13.5 miles to I-88 West. Follow I-88 West for about 24 miles to the Aurora/Batavia exit. At the end of the exit, turn onto IL-31. The Baymont Inn and Suites will be located on your right.

history

We were not able to determine much dark history in this hotel's past. This site seems to be rather modern, built as a stopping point along I-88. However, numerous people have been reporting strange things here for the last few years.

ghost story

All kinds of odd occurrences happen in this hotel. People hear voices and footsteps. Objects move by themselves, and doors open and close without anyone touching them. Figures are said to pass through the hallways, only to vanish.

On St. Patrick's Day 2001, a guest was on the phone at around 2 a.m. when suddenly, a mysterious ball of light purportedly emerged from behind the lobby desk, and then floated around briefly before vanishing.

On another occasion, a guest called the front desk in the middle of the night to complain about people talking too loudly in the room next to him. The employee checked the records and discovered that no one had checked into that room. However, this hotel employee came upstairs and heard the voices too. But as soon as he opened the door, the voices ceased, and he discovered that the room was completely empty.

On another occasion, a guest came down to the lobby in the middle of the night completely terrified. He was staying in Room 208 and reported that he woke up in the middle of the night feeling like someone was strangling him. There was no one else in the room.

visiting

In order to check out the ghosts at the Baymont, you must get a room for the night. There is no option to just roam the building looking for ghosts without actually renting a room because this is an operating business. However, rooms are reasonably priced. The ghosts are most active in the middle of the night, most often appearing long after midnight.

BIOGRAPH THEATER

2433 North Lincoln Avenue, Chicago, Illinois 60614

directions

The Biograph Theater is located in downtown Chicago, just north of the city's center. Take North LaSalle Street north for about 2 miles. Turn left onto North Clark Street, then left onto North Lincoln Avenue. After about 1 mile, you will see the Biograph Theater on your right. The haunted alley is on the southeast side of the theater.

history

After the FBI threatened to have a London woman named Anna Sage deported unless she helped them catch notorious bank robber and murderer John Dillinger, Sage agreed to lure an unsuspecting Dillinger to the Biograph Theater for an FBI ambush. She told FBI agents that she would wear a bright red dress while accompanying Dillinger, so that they would know where he was as patrons exited the movie.

After watching a movie called *Manhattan Melodrama*, Sage exited the Biograph with a young man wearing a hat and a pinstriped suit. FBI agent Melvin Purvis walked up to the man and advised him that he was surrounded. Purvis advised that he surrender because there was no way that he could escape. In a panic, the man fled and turned down an alley beside the Biograph, where he was gunned down by the FBI.

The man was taken to a nearby hospital where he was pronounced dead. His body was then moved to the Cook County Morgue, where hundreds came to see John Dillinger's body. The blood-soaked alley beside the Biograph was also inundated with souvenir hunters as people used handkerchiefs to sop up the famous bank robber's blood.

However, some suggest that the body that was moved to the morgue wasn't John Dillinger's at all. They suggest that Sage had warned Dillinger of the plot and had instead fooled a lookalike to pose as Dillinger at the Biograph. The dead man had different color eyes than Dillinger. There were missing scars. His height and build also varied from that of Dillinger.

Whoever the dead man was, once the souvenir hunters sopped up the final drop of his blood, something else remained in that alley.

ghost story

The alley where Dillinger reportedly died is reputed to be a haunted place. Most of the reports about this alley are vague. People feel uncomfortable or scared when walking through the alley, especially at night. Other times, cold breezes inexplicably blow or a spot of cold air will hover in the middle of the alley.

While these strange temperature fluctuations and emotions are the most common paranormal experiences in this alley, others claim to have seen the ghost of Dillinger himself running through it. People report seeing a man run down the alley and fall to the ground before vanishing. The figure appears transparent, with a blue tint. The apparition appears exclusively at night.

visiting

While the Biograph itself is only open certain hours of the day, it is not the Biograph that is haunted. The ghost stories take place in the alley beside the Biograph. This alley is open throughout the night and is completely accessible to anyone brave enough to face the ghost of John Dillinger.

CANTIGNY

1S151 South Winfield Road, Wheaton, Illinois 60189

directions

From the center of Chicago, take I-290 West for about 14 miles to I-88 West. Follow I-88 West for a little more than 6 miles to the Highland Avenue exit. Keep right on the exit ramp and then turn right onto Highland Avenue. Immediately merge onto the Butterfield Road ramp on the left and follow Butterfield road for a little more than 8 miles. Turn right onto Winfield Road and follow that for a little more than 1.5 miles. Cantigny will be on your right.

history

Cantigny was originally a large estate owned by Joseph Medill and, eventually, Joseph's grandson Colonel Robert McCormick. McCormick named the estate Cantigny after the World War I battle of the same name, in which he participated. While living at the estate, McCormick was married twice. His first wife, Amy, did not have any children. His second wife, Maryland, had two children from a previous marriage named Ann and Alice.

When McCormick died in 1955, he left his money to charity and stated that the estate would be made into a park. This soon came to pass. Two buildings on the property were made into museums. One of the buildings is a military museum and the other—McCormick's original, 35-room mansion—was also restored and made into a museum. The grounds were repurposed as parkland, a large 27-hole golf course, and a tank park that displays many military tanks.

McCormick and his first wife, Amy, are buried on the grounds.

ghost story

Two young girls haunt Cantigny. According to legend, these two girls were the children of McCormick's second wife. Most often, the girls are said to tinker with the lights in the mansion. Even when the building is empty, lights mysteriously turn on and off. When the lights turn on and the house is investigated, no one who could have turned on the lights can be found.

Visitors to Cantigny are sometimes approached by the girls as well. A young girl is said to approach visitors and tell them about the grounds and how her father owns the property. She explains how much she loves her property and Cantigny, then runs off behind a building. When the visitor investigates around the back of the building, they find no girl present, and no explicable place where she could have disappeared to.

visiting

You many only enter the grounds of Cantigny when they are open to the public. The museums and grounds are free to the public, but parking costs $5 per car. The grounds are open 9 a.m.–sunset November–April 30, with the exception of January, when the grounds are closed. The grounds are open 7 a.m.–sunset May 1–October 31. You will need to roam the grounds during this time period and wait for a little girl to approach you, telling you everything about life and death at Cantigny.

CHICAGO WATER TOWER

800 North Michigan Avenue, Chicago, Illinois 60611

directions

Located near the center of Chicago, the water tower is 8 blocks north on Michigan Avenue. It is located at the northeast corner of the intersection of Michigan Avenue and Chicago Avenue.

history

On October 8, 1871, Chicago caught fire. The dry conditions and wooden construction of the city allowed the fire to spread quickly and rage powerfully. The fire devastated the city, destroying much of its densely populated center. At least 300 people were killed in the disaster, and more than 100,000 people were left homeless in its aftermath.

The Chicago Water Tower was one of the few buildings in the city that was not constructed primarily of wood. It was designed by architect William Boyington and constructed out of limestone, making it one of the stronger structures in the city. As the fire raged around the water tower, many of the workers there fled for their lives. One heroic worker decided to stay behind to help fight the fire. The worker diligently worked the pumps to combat the blaze.

Despite his best efforts, the blaze advanced ever closer to the water tower and eventually surrounded it, leaving the worker no place to escape. To spare himself from death by fire, the worker hanged himself on the upper level of the building.

The water tower survived the fire.

ghost story

Back in the early days of the city, a man named Captain Streeter made a claim on the land where the water tower sits today. But the land was taken from him by the state of Illinois. Enraged, Streeter cursed the property. Some say that the strange things that occur here are due to this curse.

People report hearing voices and burning fires even when they are alone and nothing nearby is burning. Objects are said to move by themselves. All manner of odd things occur here.

The most famous ghost appears in the upstairs window of the water tower. Witnesses report seeing a man in the upstairs window that has hanged himself.

Many of these witnesses are so convinced of what they see, that they scream or run to tell others. Once, a group of tourists saw the figure and went to grab a police officer. The police officer came and saw the hanging figure too.

visiting

The water tower is open to the public and is free to enter. It is open 10 a.m.-6:30 p.m. daily except on Sunday, when it is open 10 a.m.-5 p.m. The sightings of the hanging man are often seen from the exterior of the building. You can stand outside the building any time of the day or night. Most of the sightings take place around the anniversary of the blaze in October.

COLONEL PALMER HOUSE

660 East Terra Cotta Avenue, Crystal Lake, Illinois 60014

directions

From the center of Chicago, take I-90 West for about 26.5 miles to the Roselle Road exit. Keep right on the exit and merge onto North Roselle Road. Follow this for 1 mile before turning left onto West Algonquin Road. Follow this road for 13 miles and then turn right onto North Mail Street/IL-31. Follow IL-31 for about 6 miles, then turn left onto Terra Cotta Avenue. The Colonel Palmer House will be on the right after about 0.5 mile.

history

The Colonel Palmer House was built by Colonel Gustavus Palmer and his wife, Henrietta, in 1858. Colonel Palmer was an important member of the Crystal Lake community, and many community gatherings and events were held within his house, which was quite large for that era. Throughout the remainder of their lives, the Palmers used the house as a farmhouse.

The Palmers lived in the house for 26 years until December 1884, when both of them caught typhoid pneumonia. Both died from the disease, within days of each other.

The house passed ownership to Colonel Palmer's son, who owned the home for a few more years before passing away himself around the turn of the century. The house was then rented out and used for different purposes throughout the next few decades.

According to some accounts, during these years, the house was used as an orphanage. The orphanage was run by a cruel man who often beat the children who lived there. Some stories suggest that the man beat some of the children so severely that he killed them. He stored their bodies in the basement until he was able to dispose of them. The basement was also where particularly ill-behaved children were locked up after beating.

In 1979, the house was donated to the City of Crystal Lake. It was restored and today houses the headquarters of the Crystal Lake Historical Society.

ghost story

Whether or not the house's use as an orphanage and its dark past are true, the building does seem to be haunted by small children. Much of the activity manifests through sounds. People hear children crying within the house, even when there are no children anywhere inside or nearby. People hear what sounds like children stomping on floors or scratching on doors.

While these sounds occur throughout the building, the most haunted part of the house is reportedly its basement. An exterior cellar door leads to the basement and it is said that if you place your ear to the door after dark, you can hear banging. Some say that this is a replay of the beatings that once took place in the basement. Others have reported seeing the sad faces of small children in the windows of the basement. Sometimes, people take pictures of the building and later examine the photographs only to find what appear to be faces in the basement windows.

visiting

Three days a week, the building is open to the public for tours. On Tuesdays, it is open 3–7 p.m. On Thursdays and Fridays, it is open 11 a.m.–4 p.m. The house is also open for private events, for which days and times vary.

If you want to approach the house when it is closed, do so with caution. You may be able to approach the exterior to take pictures of the basement window or even place your ear to the cellar door. I would suggest not trying this at night. You may be stopped or even arrested, as neighbors will likely report the presence of trespassers around the abandoned building at night.

CONGRESS HOTEL

520 South Michigan Avenue, Chicago, Illinois 60605

directions

The Congress Hotel is near the center of Chicago at the intersection of Michigan Avenue and Congress Parkway. The hotel is a couple blocks from the lake and overlooks Grant Park.

history

The hotel was a grand structure built to cater to attendees of Chicago's 1893 World's Fair. Throughout its many years of operation, countless famous individuals have stayed at the hotel, including movie stars and several Presidents of the United States.

Some say that the Congress Hotel had become a headquarters for Al Capone during his reign as crime lord during Prohibition, although there is little evidence to support this theory.

Another rumor suggests that it is the inspiration behind Stephen King's short story 1408. In this story, a writer who pens ghost stories stays in a hotel that supposedly has a room so haunted, no one will stay in it. During the one night he lodges there, he experiences the most terrifying moments of his life.

ghost story

Several rooms throughout the hotel are considered haunted. The most haunted room that is still open to the public is room 441. Many strange things happen in this room, including the sound of voices, manifestations of apparitions, the presence of cold

spots, and poltergeist activity that includes objects launching themselves across the room. There is also rumored to be a room on the hotel's 12th floor that is so haunted, it is actually closed to the public and hidden from view. The doorway is said to have been permanently sealed and wallpaper installed over it.

The Florentine Room was once a roller-skating rink. Today, people still hear the sounds of roller skates crossing the floor, as well as those of organ music. People on the fifth floor of the building often hear moans near the elevator. Throughout the common areas of the hotel, objects are said to throw themselves across the room. Cold spots and apparitions are also felt and seen throughout the hotel, especially after dark.

Another haunted room in the hotel, the Gold Room, is frequently used for events and weddings. A strange phenomenon often appears in wedding photographs. People who are known to have been present in pictures are mysteriously absent in the final photographs. There are blank spots in the photographs where the people were standing, and no one can explain why they are not there. The mysterious photographs are most often taken near the grand piano in the Gold Room.

The most famous apparition in the building is named Peg Leg Johnny and belongs to a homeless man who was killed at the hotel. People report seeing a haggard, one-legged man in the south tower of the hotel who mysteriously vanishes into thin air upon being approached.

visiting

Due to its tony location and grand view, it is rather pricey to stay at this hotel for the night. But actually booking a room is really the only way to explore and perhaps experience its ghosts. If you do choose to stay at the hotel, you can ask to reserve room 441, if it is available. The hotel is beautiful, convenient to many attractions, and offers amazing views of Michigan Avenue and the lake. If you can afford a night here, it is well worth the money. Beyond this, the décor makes it feel as though you are entering a different time and place.

EDGEWATER ATHLETIC CLUB

1040 West Granville Avenue, Chicago, Illinois 60660

directions

From the center of Chicago, take Lake Shore Drive to the north for about 6 miles to Sheridan Road. Follow Sheridan for a little more than 0.5 mile, then turn left onto West Granville Avenue. The Edgewater Athletic Club is inside an apartment complex located a little more than 1 block down the road, at the intersection with Kenmore Avenue.

history

This building was once one of the grandest hotels in all of Chicago. Called the Sovereign Hotel, it towered over Kenmore Avenue and displayed stunning views of Lake Michigan. Some of the most powerful people of the time stayed here. Al Capone was documented to have stayed here on occasion, as did Charlie Chaplin and even the king of Denmark.

Today, the building is composed mostly of apartments. The only exception is the area designated as the Edgewater Athletic Club, a private facility that includes a weight-training room at the site of the Sovereign's former grand ballroom. The architecture of the space appears much as it did when the Sovereign was still a hotel.

A few years ago, a student from nearby Loyola University lived in the apartments that are currently within the old hotel. The student jumped from his upper-story window to his death.

ghost story

The entrance to the athletic club is actually on Kenmore Avenue, and as you enter the door, you will be greeted by an admittedly creepy picture of the hotel staff from the early 20th century. The entire athletic club has the same eerie feeling throughout. Many employees have admitted feeling "creeped out" from time to time. Some have experienced phenomena for which they have no explanation.

Employees witness a punching bag in the club seeming to move back and forth by itself. Exercise balls sometimes launch across the room when there is no one nearby. Fire alarms go off for no reason, at all hours of the day or night. Strange atmospheric phenomena occur throughout the building as well. The temperature is said to spike or drop dramatically for no reason, then return to normal as if nothing had occurred. A stairwell near where the student killed himself sometimes exhibits high electromagnetic readings, an indication, according to some paranormal investigators, that there is ghostly activity in the vicinity.

Apparitions are often seen throughout the athletic club as well. They take the form of ballroom dancers who move throughout the hallways and the ballroom of the building.

visiting

The club is open on weekdays, 5:30 a.m.–10 p.m., and on weekends, 8 a.m.–8 p.m. You do not have to be a member to enter, but you do have to purchase a $12 day pass to experience the ghostly activity inside the building. Mention ghosts to the staff, and they will often happily recount some of their own experiences with the building's ghosts.

FORD CENTER FOR THE PERFORMING ARTS ORIENTAL THEATRE'S DEATH ALLEY

24 West Randolph Street, Chicago, Illinois 60601

directions

The Oriental Theatre is located in the center of Chicago, two blocks east of City Hall on West Randolph Street. While some of the hauntings occur within the theater itself, other hauntings happen outside the theater in a small alley behind it. Many know this place as Death Alley.

history

The Oriental Theatre was once known as the Iroquois Theater, and when it opened in 1903, it was considered cutting-edge in terms of fire safety technology. Huge asbestos curtains were designed to protect the audience from any disasters on stage, and an unheard-of 25 exits were constructed to allow the theater to empty quickly in case of disaster. When the theater opened in November 1903, many planned pieces of fire safety equipment had not yet been acquired. There was no sprinkler system or fire alarm. Furthermore, much of the interior construction was made of wood, and the seat cushions were made from hemp. Still, the theater was billed as "absolutely fireproof." But it's never a good idea to tempt fate.

On December 30, about a month after the theater opened, an overflow crowd of about 2,000 people packed inside it. At the beginning of the second act, sparks flew from one of the light fixtures and the theater caught fire. At first, the audience thought that it was part of the show, but soon they panicked. Due to the building's wooden interior structure and hemp seat cushions, the fire spread quickly. Then the lights went out. When the blinded and panicked patrons reached the doors, they discovered another fatal design flaw: The doors swung inward. As people tried to open them, the crush of panicked others behind them pushed them against the exits. They were unable to open the doors, many of which were locked. Hundreds of people were trapped inside the building.

One of the upstairs exits led to what was meant to be a fire escape. But as the patrons stepped out the door, they realized that the escape had not been completed.

There was only a metal platform, teetering about 100 feet above the ground with no stairs to descend from it. Painters working across the alley saw what was happening and quickly constructed a bridge from ladders and boards for the trapped people to cross. The bridge saved as many as 12 people, but many more died. Some jumped 10 stories to the cobblestones below, but most were crushed by the panicked masses crowding the exits. A pile of at least 150 dead bodies lay in the alley below the unfinished fire escape.

All told, at least 603 people were killed in the fire. This alone makes it the deadliest single structure fire in American history. And yet, there are some indications that not all of the deaths were reported because many bodies were removed from the scene.

ghost story

The theater is haunted by memories of this terrible day in American history. People report seeing apparitions within the theater, most commonly in the form of an angel in its upper levels. This could be the ghost of Nellie Reed, one of the five employees who died in the fire. She was an aerialist who was playing a fairy in the play and was supposed to fly out over the audience, dropping flowers upon them. During the fire, she fell from her perch above the stage and died due to injuries from the fall and the fire.

The back alley of the theater where at least 150 people fell to their deaths has earned the moniker "death alley." It is haunted. Few people can walk through the alley at night without experiencing feelings of dread and discomfort. These feelings are also apparent during daylight hours. But they aren't the only paranormal phenomena that occur here. Witnesses report hearing distant screams both inside of the theater and in "death alley." Perhaps the most unsettling incidents to occur here are reported as hands grabbing passersby by the ankles and legs as they walk through the area where most of the victims fell to their deaths.

visiting

The theater is only open to the public for performances. The performance schedule is subject to change and is available for viewing online. The theater becomes quite busy during performances, though, so you may find it difficult to experience paranormal activity during these times.

"Death alley" is open throughout the night. You can go to the haunted alley at any time to look for ghosts. Make sure that if you go here, you exercise proper caution and not go alone into this dark and creepy alleyway.

HOTEL BAKER

100 West Main Street, St. Charles, Illinois 60174

directions

From the center of Chicago, take I-290 for about 16.5 miles to Exit 13B, the IL-64 West exit. Follow IL-64 West for about 20.5 miles into St. Charles. The Hotel Baker will be on your right. It's a five-story, brown structure with a central tower and is located right next to the river.

history

In 1919, a business known as Haines Mill, which sat on this site, caught fire. The fire burned destructively and completely. The mill was destroyed. For the next seven years, the site was simply used as a garbage dump for the town. In 1926, a man named Colonel Baker was unwilling to stand for a garbage dump in the middle of his town, so he bought the land and built a hotel. The hotel was completed in 1928 and boasted many modern amenities. It was built with its own hydroelectric power generator, powered by the adjacent Fox River. It had a modern telephone system and a lighted dance floor. There was a parking garage next door to the hotel and a radio station in the tower that is today the penthouse suite.

In the early days of the hotel, a chambermaid fell desperately in love with another employee at the hotel. They soon became engaged. One day, the chambermaid went to bed on the sixth floor of the hotel (today the penthouse) where she lived, while her fiancé stayed downstairs to play a late-night game of poker. After the poker game, her fiancé disappeared. Crushed, the chambermaid was able to do nothing but cry for hours on end. This continued for a few weeks until, one day, she was seen wandering around listlessly by the river. She disappeared that night, never to be seen again. Many assume that she jumped into the river and drowned.

ghost story

It seems that the ghost of the chambermaid haunts the hotel to this day. Throughout the hotel, guests and employees have reported hearing the sounds of crying. If the witnesses to this sobbing search for its source, they never find it. Many times, this crying goes on for extended periods of time and those who listen to the crying begin to feel melancholy themselves.

The chambermaid's ghost is also known to mess with the bedding throughout the hotel. Sometimes, a bed will become messed up despite it having been made earlier and no one having entered the room. Other times, the linens and bedding will crumple and move, sometimes pulling themselves off of the bed entirely while terrified witnesses are lying in the bed.

visiting

The most haunted section of the hotel is the penthouse on the sixth floor of the building. People say that this is because the chambermaid lived here when she was staying at the hotel. In order to gain access to this area, though, you will need to rent a room there. Ghostly activity is reported throughout the rest of the hotel, as well, so renting any room may expose you to a haunting. If you did not want to stay for the night, you may visit the hotel's restaurant and bar instead.

HOUSE OF BLUES

329 North Dearborn, Chicago, Illinois 60654

directions

The House of Blues is located near the center of Chicago, on the north shore of the Chicago River. Take North Dearborn Street over the Chicago River. The House of Blues will be on your right.

history

Originally, the House of Blues and the building next to it, the Hotel Sax, were office buildings that were turned into the music venue and hotel.

In the early years of the Hotel Sax, a little girl died there. She was very ill when she came to Chicago, and she stayed at the hotel during her last days. She was known to all who went to see her as a very happy little girl, despite her debilitating illness and condition. Eventually, she succumbed to the illness, as those close to her knew she would. She died in the hotel, saddening all who had grown close to her during her stay.

ghost story

The House of Blues and the Hotel Sax are haunted by the ghost of the little girl who died in the hotel. Those who have experienced her or felt her presence report that she is a very happy and playful spirit. She apparently also likes practical jokes.

The ghost of the little girl is experienced throughout the buildings, not restricted to any particular room of the hotel, but moving throughout most of its rooms, as well as the House of Blues. The girl is said to lock doors that were not supposed to be locked. People's shoelaces sometimes come untied suddenly, as if some unseen force has suddenly tugged on them. An imprint of a small girl is reported to appear in fresh bedsheets, even when no one has been lying there. Audio recordings have captured a little girl's voice saying, "Play with me."

The little girl is seen and experienced most often when there is a little boy around age 7 or 8 in the vicinity. It seems that the little girl likes to play with boys her own age.

visiting

Your best bet for experiencing the ghost of the little girl is to actually book a hotel room for the night. Most of the activity attributed to this little girl has been experienced in the hotel rooms themselves, and there is not a specific room that experiences more activity than another. Bathroom doors are said to lock when there is no one inside, and the imprint of a little girl is said to appear on bedsheets. If you do not have the time or the money to stay at the hotel, you can still experience the ghost in the House of Blues, which is a music venue and bar. You must visit the venue's website, to view details and pricing for upcoming events.

HUNTLEY GREASE FACTORY
11822 Powder Park Road, Huntley, Illinois 60142

directions
From the center of Chicago, take I-90 West for a little more than 45 miles to the IL-47 exit toward Woodstock. Take IL-47 North toward Woodstock and follow this for about 2.5 miles to Dean Street. Turn right onto Dean Street and follow this route for about 0.5 mile before turning right onto Martin Drive. Follow this route to Powder Park Road. Turn right onto Powder Park Road. The road will veer to the right. At this juncture, you will see an unnamed dirt road. Keep left and follow the dirt road for about 100 yards to the abandoned factory. The factory is located just south of the dirt road.

history
This abandoned factory was originally the Fencil Fuze Factory in the 1940s, used to manufacture detonator caps during World War II. The work was quite dangerous due to the nature of the explosives that were used in the manufacturing, so the pay was good. The only accident in the factory occurred in 1945, when a single explosion seriously injured two people.

The darker history behind the factory is based on the quality of product that it released. The fuses that this factory created were eventually considered faulty, and they were blamed for 38 American deaths and 127 American injuries.

After the plant was shut down, many of the workers who had lost their jobs had nowhere else to go. Many of them were left homeless and took up residence within the abandoned factory. After a while, many of these homeless people moved elsewhere, and the factory became even more empty. Due to its seclusion, people began using the building as a site to commit suicide. Sometimes, the bodies of those who killed themselves would sit for weeks before anyone found them.

ghost story

The factory is haunted by apparitions of the employees who used to work here. People report seeing figures working within the building. These figures carry on as if the factory is still operational, then eventually fade away into nothingness. People who have made audio recordings within the building and the surrounding area have captured strange voices and sounds that were not audible when the recording was made. These voices and sounds seem to capture the clamor of a factory. People who have brought pets into the area report their pets acting strangely and not wanting to enter the building.

visiting

From what we were able to determine at the time of this writing, this site is not private property and therefore not closed to the public at any time. Even so, rules governing a specific location can change at any time. If you approach the area and find signs that warn you not to trespass, enter, or anything along these lines, do not continue any farther.

Once you manage to find the factory (it is difficult to find and should be scouted during daylight hours only), there are other things to keep in mind. The secluded building is a creepy example of urban decay. The walls are falling in and the entire building is decrepit. There are ways to enter the building itself and the graffiti inside suggests that many have. This structure is very unsafe and you should not enter the building. A wall or floor could collapse at any time, as there has been no upkeep since the middle of the last century. Our recommendation is that you look inside the building from an exterior vantage point but do not enter.

JANE ADDAMS' HULL HOUSE MUSEUM
800 South Halsted Street, Chicago, Illinois 60607

directions

The Hull House Museum is located near the center of Chicago. To reach it, drive south on LaSalle Street to Adams Street, then turn right. Follow Adams Street for about 0.75 mile to South Halsted Street and turn left. The Hull House Museum will be on your right.

history

The Hull Mansion was originally constructed in 1856. At the time, the area was one of the most affluent places in the city, a site where its richest men built their mansions. This changed in 1871, when the Great Chicago Fire decimated the city. After the Great Chicago Fire, the rich citizens who lived here sold their homes and moved elsewhere. Charles Hull gave the building to his niece Helen Carver, who allowed the building to be run as a retirement home by the Little Sisters of the Poor, who housed poor, working-class immigrants and the elderly, many of whom died in the house.

In 1889, Helen Carver granted the building to Jane Addams, who wanted to use it as a part of a grand social experiment. While the community was overrun by prostitution and murder, Addams wanted to create a "voice of humanity" amid the squalor.

Addams' experiment set up a place for learning and social wellbeing in the middle of one of the worst parts of town. The Hull House provided classes in arts and humanities to those in the community. A daycare and country club were set up for the poor at a time when parents would tie their children to bedposts while they went to work for the day. The Hull House was a beacon of hope in an almost hopeless environment.

In 1913, a story began circulating about a man who brazenly declared that he would rather have a portrait of the devil in his house than a portrait of the Virgin Mary. The man supposedly had a child who was born with horns and pointed ears as well as scaly skin and a tail. Terrified, he anonymously dropped the child off at the Hull House. The story goes on to say that Addams attempted to have the child baptized, but things went horribly awry during the event. Thus, Addams locked the child in the attic.

Upon hearing the story, Addams would laugh and say it was completely fabricated. When asked about other ghosts in the house, though skeptical at first, she eventually admitted to witnessing several paranormal events.

ghost story

Jane Addams was convinced that the front bedrooms on the second floor of the Hull House were haunted. Objects would move without explanation and people would hear strange sounds coming from the bedrooms. Addams herself experienced an apparition of a ghostly woman in white in one of the front bedrooms. The same woman was seen by numerous others throughout the long history of the Hull House.

Apparitions, phantom footsteps, items moving, and all varieties of ghostly activity have occurred in the building. Some say that the activity is caused by the wife of Charles Hull, who died in the house in 1860. Others say that the ghosts are those of the elderly who passed away in the house when it was a retirement home in the 1870s.

The attic is reputedly the most haunted place in the building. Although Addams laughed and adamantly denied the stories about the devil child that was housed in the attic, to this day some people believe that the story is true. While the stories about the genesis of the devil child are likely fabricated, many believe that there was really a

terribly deformed child who was hidden away in the attic of the building. These beliefs are bolstered by those who claim to see the face of a deformed child looking down at them from the attic window.

visiting

Tuesday–Friday, the building is open 10 a.m.–4 p.m. as a museum. On Sunday, it is open noon–4 p.m. The building is closed on Mondays and Saturdays. Admission is free to the museum, so if you are able to visit the building during regular business hours, it is well worth your time to explore the history and hauntings of the interior of the Hull House. If you are not able to visit during regular business hours, you still can stand on the street outside of the building and gaze up toward the attic window, hoping to catch a glimpse of the "devil child."

JOHN HANCOCK CENTER

875 North Michigan Avenue, Chicago, Illinois 60611

directions

John Hancock Center is located near the center of Chicago. To get there, take Michigan Avenue north over the Chicago River. John Hancock Center is a large skyscraper that sits on Michigan Avenue between Delaware Place and Chestnut Street.

history

Captain Streeter, a land owner who lived in Chicago during the early 1900s, believed that he owned the land that John Hancock Center stands upon today. The city of Chicago disagreed, and a long legal battle ensued, lasting until Streeter's death in the 1920s. On his deathbed, angry about the legal proceedings that had taken his time and attempted to take his property, he cursed the land so that no one would ever be happy there again.

Since the construction of the immense skyscraper was completed in 1968, several strange and unexpected tragedies have occurred in the building. The first strange event occurred just three years after the tower's completion, when 29-year-old Lorraine Kowalski broke through the glass and fell from the 90th floor of the building. Investigators were perplexed by the event because the window that she broke through was strong enough to withstand the brutal Chicago winds.

After this event, several more strange deaths occurred on the upper floors of the building. In 1975, a radio station employee fell from the 97th floor of the building to his death. That same year, a 27-year-old student fell from the 91st floor. Upon investigation, the student appeared to have been studying over breakfast when he fell. In 1978, a 31-year-old woman shot a man on the 65th floor of the building. In 1998, comedian and actor Chris Farley was found dead near his 60th-floor apartment from an apparent drug overdose. Finally, in 2002, a section of scaffold fell from the building's 43rd floor for no apparent reason, landing on 11 people, 3 of whom died. These were not the only deaths to occur at the building, but many of these deaths seemed quite inexplicable.

Anton LaVey, the founder of the Church of Satan and a famous occultist, attributed the strange deaths to the building's trapezoidal shape. In his research into the occult, LaVey posited that "strange angles" in architecture cause bizarre actions from otherwise ordinary people. Since the shape of the building is trapezoidal, the exterior walls of the building are not situated at 90-degree angles. LaVey stated that the building was essentially a portal to hell and a center of "dark energy."

ghost story

Some say that demons haunt this building due to its shape and "dark energy." Many of the stories about this building involve people feeling uncomfortable or not quite like themselves while inside. People sometimes feel as if they are not in complete control of their own actions, or they will lose balance or feel ill for no apparent reason. Some have suggested that the strange deaths are due to these feelings people experience while within the building's walls.

A few stories circulate about shadowy figures and demonic voices on the upper floors of the building and observation deck. These stories are much less prevalent than those about visitors feeling bizarre and almost possessed while inside.

visiting

The building offers tours 9 a.m.–11 p.m. daily. This is probably the best way to visit and explore the colossal building. The John Hancock Center houses a variety of businesses and apartments. Technically, the building is always open, but there are security guards in the building who will make you leave if you do not have a legitimate reason to be there. Unfortunately, looking for ghosts is likely not considered a good reason.

LELAND TOWER SUITES

7 South Stolp Avenue, Aurora, Illinois 60505

directions

From the center of Chicago, take I-290 West for a little more than 13.5 miles to I-88 West. Follow I-88 West for about 24 miles to the Aurora/Batavia exit. Turn right at the end of the exit onto IL-31 and follow this road for about 2.5 miles before turning left onto West Galena Boulevard. Follow this route across the river. The Leland Tower is the largest building on the island and is located at the corner of Stolp Avenue by the river.

history

In 1926, an ambitious project was started in Aurora, Illinois. A grand hotel was built, slated to be the largest building and the most modern hotel in all of Illinois, outside of

Chicago. The tower was completed two years later, in 1928, and soared to 22 stories, dominating the skyline of Aurora. For a while, it was a successful hotel. Several famous people stayed here due to modern amenities such as a telephone in each room. Sally Rand, Phillip Wrigley, and Gene Autry all slept within this tower.

By the 1960s, the hotel fell on hard times and the business was forced to shutter. For a while, the tower and the transmitter atop it were used as the headquarters for an Aurora television station. Eventually, this, too, left the building. Today, the building is an apartment complex.

Somehow, perhaps due to its height and dominance in Aurora's skyline, the building has become a destination for people who want to commit suicide. Several residents of the building, as well as others from the city, chose this as the site to end their lives. Numerous people have jumped from the upper floors of the building into the Fox River below.

ghost story

Several ghosts have taken up residence within this building. Many of the stories about the building involve phantom smells. People report smelling cigar or cigarette smoke within the halls and apartments, despite smoking being prohibited here. Others mention catching a whiff of decaying meat while inside the elevator.

People report hearing strange voices throughout the halls as well. When these voices are investigated, their source is never discovered.

Ghosts are often reported just outside of the building, as well. People see apparitions just outside the hotel, next to the Fox River. Sometimes, these apparitions appear completely real until they suddenly vanish, while at other times, people see transparent or wispy forms that slowly fade away.

visiting

Because this building is currently an operating apartment complex, you will be unable to enter looking for ghosts, unless you are a resident of the building itself. That being said, you may still be able to spot some ghosts at Leland Tower. There are no restrictions on searching the area outside the tower by the river, so do so to your heart's content. Your best bet for finding a ghost here is to visit after dark, as this is when the apparitions are most often seen.

MANTENO STATE HOSPITAL

3 Diversatech Drive, Manteno, Illinois 60950

directions

From the center of Chicago, take I-57 South for a little more than 31 miles to Exit 327 toward Peotone and Wilmington. Turn left onto West Wilmington Road and follow it for about 2 miles, then turn right onto Drecksler Road. Follow this route for 2 miles, then turn left onto West County Line Road. Take your first right onto North 5000E Road and follow this for a little more than 3 miles before turning right onto East 9000N Road. Follow this for another mile, then take a left onto North 4000E Road. Follow this road for about 1.25 miles, then turn right onto Diversatech Drive. This intersection was previously the front gate for the Manteno State Hospital. All of the buildings in this area once belonged to the Manteno State Hospital, including the HomeStar bank—which is contained in the "H"-shaped buildings situated two blocks to your right and left.

history

In December 1930, the first 100 patients arrived at the insane asylum called Manteno State Hospital. From this date until 1985, when the facility officially shut down, all

manner of horrible things happened to the thousands of patients who were "treated" at the facility.

Experimental treatments that are considered barbaric in many modern circles were conducted regularly at the Manteno State Hospital. Electroshock therapy was used frequently, as well as hydrotherapy, a method of placing patients briefly in freezing cold water. Lobotomies were also performed frequently at this facility.

In 1939, an epidemic of typhoid fever broke out here. More than 400 patients at the facility became ill, and as many as 60 died of the disease.

By 1954, the facility housed 8,195 patients, which was far above capacity. Only 200 employees were there to care for the patients, which meant that many of them did not receive proper care. More efforts were made to make the insane more docile than to make them better. Reports of sexual assaults later surfaced. Numerous people received experimental treatments, though they did not need them. Patients often attempted to escape, only to get lost in the adjoining cornfields, eventually to die from the elements and be found by the neighboring farmers.

The most famous case of patient mistreatment involved a woman named Gennie Pilarski, who was committed by her parents when she was only 25 because of a disagreement over her living arrangements. There is some evidence that Pilarski may have suffered from bipolar disorder, but notes from the facility state that she was friendly and agreeable and showed no signs of pathology.

Pilarski was submitted to electroshock therapy twice weekly for the next 11 years. After 11 years and more than 200 treatments, she was lobotomized, leaving her mentally handicapped. After the lobotomy, Pilarski was unable to interact with others, was unable to feed herself, and became totally dependent on her caregivers for tasks as rudimentary as using the bathroom. She lived for another 43 years, completely dependent upon others, before dying at the age of 80.

ghost story

Following all of the horror that took place here over the years, it is no wonder that negative energy has lingered. Most of the ghostly activity occurs within the buildings that still exist from the time when this hospital was active. At times, it almost seems as if the hospital is still in operation.

Apparitions have been reported all throughout the grounds. These apparitions take the form of doctors, nurses, and patients wearing clothing unique to the time period that Manteno State Hospital was in operation. These figures do not seem to notice the presence of the modern world. They ignore people, objects, and buildings that were not present on the original facility grounds.

Perhaps the creepiest paranormal occurrences here are sounds. People report hearing crying and screaming coming from within the buildings and throughout the grounds. Others report hearing voices resounding over an intercom system that no longer exists.

visiting

Unfortunately, it is nearly impossible to gain access to any of the remaining hospital buildings. Although there are reports of paranormal activity on the streets and the grounds, most of the paranormal reports pertain to the interior of the buildings themselves. Many of the buildings are owned by Veterans Affairs. The surviving buildings on the northern third of the campus have been turned into nursing facilities for veterans, and so are completely inaccessible to ghost hunters. Many of the other surviving buildings are used for storage or warehouse space. The area is owned by a variety of businesses and organizations, and none are willing to let people enter the buildings to search for ghosts.

MURDER CASTLE

611 West 63rd Street, Chicago, Illinois 60621

directions

From the center of Chicago, take I-94 East for about 7.5 miles to Exit 58B, the 63rd Street exit. Turn right onto 63rd Street. After driving a little less than 0.5 mile, you will see the post office on your left.

history

In 1886, a man named H. H. Holmes got a job as a pharmacist at a drugstore at the corner of 63rd and Wallace. The owner died of cancer, leaving the drugstore to his wife. Holmes offered to purchase the drugstore from its new owner, Mrs. Holton, but stated that he could only afford to pay her monthly. She agreed, not wanting to deal with the ownership of the store any longer. Holmes proceeded to kill her so that he would not need to pay her each month.

In 1889, Holmes had a plan to make much more money. He purchased the lot across the street from the drugstore and began building a hotel for the World's Fair, which would arrive in 1893. Simply making money off of a World's Fair hotel, however, was not enough for him. Holmes understood that many of the people who would lodge at the hotel would have great sums of money on hand and, if they were to disappear, their disappearances could not easily be traced back to him.

Holmes used many different construction companies to build the hotel. He did this so that no one would be aware of the death traps he was constructing throughout the structure. The building itself was like a maze, for which someone unfamiliar could not easily find their way out. At least 100 of the rooms in the building had no windows. Some rooms had walk-in safes with gas lines leading into them. Holmes used this method to asphyxiate his victims. There were body chutes in these rooms, as well, which led to the basement. In the basement, Holmes set up dissection tables, which he used to remove flesh from the bodies so that he could sell their skeletons to nearby medical colleges. The flesh was then thrown into his cremation furnace, which destroyed the remaining evidence.

Many of Holmes' victims were young women who he hired to work for him at the hotel and drugstore. The women were alone in the city and had come for the fair but needed a job while they were there. Holmes required the women to get life insurance policies and, after murdering them, would collect on the policies as extra profits. By the time people caught on to what Holmes had been doing and he was arrested, Holmes confessed to killing 27 people. Many people believe that this number is far too low. Some estimates suggest that as many as 200 people were killed by Holmes in the hotel that was later dubbed the Murder Castle.

Holmes' hotel was torn down eventually, and a United States Post Office branch was built on the site. Part of the Murder Castle's original foundation and basement are actually part of the existing post office.

ghost story

Some say that after Holmes was executed for his killings, he came back from the grave to kill some more. At least four of the people who were involved with Holmes' executions died under mysterious circumstances. The priest who visited him before his execution, the doctor who certified him dead, and the jury foreman on his trial all ended up dead. The superintendent of the prison where he was kept and executed committed suicide.

While the Murder Castle still stood, there were all sorts of stories about cries for help and apparitions throughout the hallways of the building. Sometimes, these sounds were even audible from outside the building. When the building was torn down and replaced with a post office, the ghost stories did not fade. People still hear cries for help. Apparitions of young women in period clothing from the time of the World's Fair are seen inside and around the post office, as well. It seems that the ghosts of Holmes' victims still walk the site where they met their ends.

visiting

The post office itself is open 8 a.m.–5 p.m. Monday–Friday, and 8 a.m.–1 p.m. Saturday. One does not necessarily need to enter the post office in order to experience the ghosts here, though. The cries for help and the apparitions have been seen around the building's exterior, as well. It is probably a bad idea to go looking for ghosts here after dark. This is not a good neighborhood, and a walk through it at night—especially with expensive equipment—could prove quite dangerous.

MUSEUM OF SCIENCE AND INDUSTRY

5700 South Lake Shore Drive, Chicago, Illinois 60637

directions

This location is about 15 minutes south of the middle of the city. Simply take Lake Shore Drive from the center of the city south for about 6.5 miles. There will be an entrance on your right called Science Drive. When Science Drive dead-ends, turn left toward the parking lot. This will bring you to the back of the Museum of Science and Industry.

history

The Museum of Science and Industry is the only surviving building from the Chicago World's Fair of 1893. It was originally the Palace of Fine Arts, and was the only structure at the fair to be built of bricks. After the fair, it became the Field Museum of Natural History, but, eventually, the natural history museum moved, leaving the structure empty. The structure remained unused for 13 years until 1933, when it became the Museum of Science and Industry. The museum houses many exhibits that accentuate technology from the past. The speedy Zephyr train is on display here, as well as the submarine U-505.

U-505 was a German submarine that was captured during World War II and was eventually purchased by the museum, which moved it to Chicago. In 1944, as this submarine was prowling the Atlantic looking for hapless Allied victims, Allied ships dropped depth charges into the water, damaging the structure and causing the future of those on board to look bleak. The commander of the boat, Peter Zschech, stood in the command room, convinced that life was over for him and his crew. He took out his pistol and shot himself in the head in front of everyone in the control room. The first officer took command and managed to steer the submarine to safety.

ghost story

Three ghosts haunt the Museum of Science and Industry. The first seems to be that of Clarence Darrow (see Clarence Darrow Memorial Bridge chapter). Darrow was a famous lawyer of his time who lived near the museum. People report seeing an elderly man wearing a suit walking throughout the museum. Those who get a close look at him report that he looks just like pictures of Clarence Darrow.

The Zephyr train is also haunted. The tour of the train includes the appearance of several animatronic figures that represent those who once worked or rode on the train. Sometimes, these figures move by themselves, despite not having been turned on. One female animatronic figure in particular is said to turn her head to look at visitors, even when she is known to be turned off.

U-505 is also haunted, supposedly by the ghost of Peter Zschech, the commander who needlessly killed himself in the command room of the submarine. People report feeling an ominous presence when they enter the submarine alone. They suddenly become sure that someone is standing behind them but turn to find no one there. Large metals doors are said to slam shut by themselves. People also sometimes see an apparition of a man in a World War II German Navy uniform who suddenly vanishes upon being seen.

visiting

While Clarence Darrow's ghost can also be seen on the grounds of Jackson Park, which surrounds the museum (see Clarence Darrow Memorial Bridge chapter), in order to see his ghost or any others inside the museum, you must pay admission and enter during regular business hours. The museum is open 9:30 a.m.–4 p.m. Monday–Friday, and 9:30 a.m.–5:30 p.m. Saturday–Sunday. Admission is $21.95 per adult; $17.95 per child.

O'HARE INTERNATIONAL AIRPORT

Bessie Coleman Drive, Chicago, Illinois 60666

directions

From the center of Chicago, take I-90 West for about 14 miles to Exit 78, the I-190 West exit. Take I-190 West for about 2.5 miles and exit to O'Hare International Airport. The exit will be listed as Departures/Upper Level T1 St. This will take you to airport parking.

history

The airport was constructed in 1942 as part of the efforts during World War II. It was originally a plant used to manufacture aircraft for the war. In 1945, the airport was no longer used for military aircraft and was renamed Orchard Field Airport. By 1949, the airport was renamed O'Hare International Airport.

As the years went by, the airport began to gain popularity. By 1961, it became the largest airport in the city, surpassing Chicago Midway International Airport.

Throughout its history, 13 planes have crashed while arriving to or departing O'Hare, killing a total of 1,057 people. The largest aircraft accident in American history occurred on May 25, 1979, when American Airlines Flight 191 crashed in a field at the end of the runway, killing all 271 people on board and 2 on the ground.

ghost story

Sometimes, people see a dramatic replay of Flight 191 in its last moments above O'Hare Airport. Witnesses report seeing a plane that appears to be veering on its side flying over the airport before disappearing toward the northwest.

While the phantom Flight 191 is perhaps the most famous ghost at the airport, there are supposedly many more apparitions that are constantly seen moving throughout the corridors of the place. Most often, people see pilots and flight attendants who mysteriously vanish into thin air. Often, these apparitions are seen wearing uniforms from the 1960s and 1970s, which set them apart from the real pilots and flight attendants walking through the corridors.

visiting

Access to the interior of the building is open to the public and free of charge. Parking will cost you money, though, and in order to access many areas of the airport, you will need to purchase an airline ticket. The phantom pilots and flight attendants are reportedly seen in the public areas of the airport, so you don't necessarily need to purchase a ticket in order to roam around looking for a ghost.

POLISH MUSEUM OF AMERICA

984 Milwaukee Avenue, Chicago, Illinois 60642

directions

From the center of Chicago, take I-90 West for a little more than 1 mile to Exit 49B, the Augusta Boulevard/Milwaukee Avenue exit. Turn left onto North Milwaukee Avenue. You will see the Polish Museum of America on your right.

history

The Polish Museum of America was built in 1935 in West Town, once a predominantly Polish neighborhood of Chicago. Having been built in 1935, Chicago's Polish Museum of America is the oldest ethnic museum in Chicago and one of the oldest ethnic museums in the entire United States. The museum has collected exhibits throughout its many years of operation, amassing enough pieces of Polish art and culture to fill the building. The building also presents numerous lectures and films.

Perhaps the most famous room within the museum is the Ignace Paderewski room. The room opened in 1941 and honors the memory of Paderewski, a famous concert pianist as well as a Polish politician—the second Prime Minister of the Republic of Poland. He died of pneumonia on June 29, 1941, in New York during a concert tour. He was buried in Warsaw, Poland.

ghost story

The Ignace Paderewski room seems to be haunted by the ghost of Paderewski himself. Some members of the cleaning crew at the museum are hesitant to enter the room at night. They state that there is something in the room that makes them uncomfortable. They report feeling like they are being watched or that something does not want them to be there late at night.

Every year on the anniversary of Paderewski's birth, November 6, and his death, June 29, flowers are placed in the room as a memorial to the great pianist. The flowers and the smell from the flowers from November 6 last long after they are placed on the fireplace mantel. However, the June 29 flowers die and rot within a day or two, perhaps reflecting that one symbolizes birth while the other symbolizes death. Others have reported strange smells coming from the room. People smell burning or food, but there is never a satisfactory explanation for these smells.

Cassette tapes have been known to turn on by themselves and play Paderewski's music, even though there was no one near the player when it starts. Other people have heard typing on the typewriter in the room, even though they can clearly see that there is no one typing on the machine.

visiting

In order to visit the Ignace Paderewski room, you must enter the museum during normal business hours. The museum is open 11 a.m.–4 p.m. Friday–Wednesday and is closed on Thursday. There is a $7 admission charge to enter the museum, and you will have to pay this in hopes of experiencing the ghost of Ignace Paderewski. The Ignace Paderewski room is located on the museum's second floor, at the top of the main stairwell.

RIALTO SQUARE THEATRE

102 North Chicago Street, Joliet, Illinois 60432

directions

From the center of Chicago, take I-55 south for about 23.5 miles to Exit 268, the South Joliet Road exit. Follow South Joliet Road for about 12.5 miles. The name of the road will change to IL-53 after about 4 miles. Turn left to follow West Ruby Street. After about 0.5 mile, the name of the road will change to North Chicago Street. Follow North Chicago Street for another 0.5 mile until you see the theater on your left.

history

This theater has a long history. It was built in 1926 to be a vaudeville movie theater, and its founders spared no expense in its construction. The lobby is lined with black-and-white marble walls. Beautiful and expensive columns decorate the building, as does a huge chandelier. The theater cost $2 million to build, an absolutely staggering amount of money in 1926.

During its many years of existence, the theater began to fall into a rather decrepit state. The building was no longer the magnificent movie palace that it had once been. In 1980, it was decided that the building would be restored to its former glory. Restoration work on the theater was successful, and today the theater hosts plays, concerts, and comedy acts. It is listed on the National Register of Historic Places.

During the early days of the theater, a man and a woman were sitting in the front row of the balcony. Somehow, while looking over the balcony to the crowd below, the man slipped over the side of the balcony. Grasping blindly for something to stop his fall, he grabbed the woman and pulled her over the balcony with him. They both died.

ghost story

Some unsuspecting visitors to the theater report feeling someone tap them on the shoulder. They turn around only to find that there is no one behind them. Besides getting poked from time to time by a phantom finger, witnesses to the paranormal activity here report also feeling freezing cold spots in the air that manifest for no natural reason. Strange noises are also heard throughout the theater, especially after close. When these noises are investigated, no source is ever found. Objects also move by themselves.

While all of these incidents happen often throughout the theater, the most famous ghosts at the Rialto are three apparitions. The first apparition is of a young, attractive woman who floats throughout the theater. She hovers slightly above the floor and glows with a hazy whitish light. Although she was seen most often while the theater was being restored in 1980, she is still spotted from time to time to this day.

The other two apparitions are of a man and woman on the balcony, supposedly in the same spot where the couple fell to their deaths in the early days of the theater. People report seeing the couple sitting alone on the balcony before suddenly disappearing.

visiting

The only way to experience the ghosts of the Rialto is to actually enter the theater. There are a couple of ways to do this. You can either purchase tickets to one of the theater's many shows, or you can purchase tickets to the theater's daily tours. The tour and show schedule are always subject to change, so check the theater's website for further details.

SHERATON GATEWAY SUITES HOTEL AT O'HARE

6501 North Mannheim Road, Rosemont, Illinois 60018

directions

From the center of Chicago, take I-90 West for about 14 miles to Exit 78, the I-190 West exit. Take I-190 West for about 1.5 miles to Exit 2A, the Mannheim Road exit. The Sheraton will be on your right.

history

There seems to be a certain amount of depression that follows people who stay at this hotel. It is frequented by business travelers who visit Chicago via O'Hare International Airport. Many of those who stay here stay alone. Some let this loneliness destroy them.

Suicides occur relatively frequently at this hotel. At least three deaths have occurred within the hotel or the adjacent parking lot from drug overdoses. But drug overdoses aren't the preferred method of suicide at this hotel. The hotel is 11 stories tall, and many people have chosen to go up to the 11th floor and jump to their deaths.

ghost story

Many of the people who stay at this hotel have heard strange noises throughout the night. Banging, voices, screaming, and crying have all been heard. Those who hear the sounds assume that they are coming from an adjacent room or from outside. This is unlikely, though, because the hotel has taken special precautions to completely soundproof each room. This was done because of the adjacent airport. Those in the hotel should not be able to hear any sounds coming from outside of their rooms.

Employees who work at the hotel overnight have heard strange sounds in the lobby in the middle of the night, especially when there is no one else around. The employees report hearing people talking, or the sounds of typing, but find no one in the lobby who could be making the sounds.

Once, a woman latched the door to her room and walked into the bathroom to take a shower. When she came out of the shower, all of her clothes had been removed from her suitcases and strewn all around the room. There was no way that anyone could have entered because the door was still latched.

People have seen the figure of a man wearing a suit standing on a balcony on the top floor of the hotel. Many times, the figure just disappears without walking back into the room. The balcony that he is seen on was actually the site where a man in a suit leapt to his death in 2001.

visiting

To experience the ghosts inside the Sheraton, you will have to rent a room and spend the night in the haunted hotel. The interior ghost experiences tend to happen late at night. However, the man in the suit on the top-floor balcony is more often seen during the day, and he can be spotted from outside.

APPENDIX I
CHAPTERS ORGANIZED GEOGRAPHICALLY

North Side:
Ford Center for the Performing Arts
Oriental Theatre's Death Valley
Hooters on Wells Street
John Hancock Center
Chicago Water Tower
House of Blues
Eastland Disaster Site
Excalibur Nightclub
Bucktown Pub
Polish Museum of America
Read Dunning Memorial Park
Webster's Wine Bar
California Clipper
Biograph Theater
Wrigley Field
Calvary Cemetery
Edgewater Athletic Club
Edgewater Lounge
Fireside Lounge
Rosehill Cemetery
Green Mill Cocktail Lounge
Graceland Cemetery
Magic Hedge
St. Valentine's Day Massacre Site
Tonic Room
Metro and Smart Bar
Drinkingbird
Gold Star Bar
Liar's Club
Clark Street Ale House
Death Corner in Little Hell

South Side:
Congress Hotel
Jane Addams' Hull House Museum
Oak Hill Cemetery and the Demon
Butcher
Clarence Darrow Memorial Bridge
Museum of Science and Industry
Murder Castle
Camp Douglas
Oak Woods Cemetery
Ethyl's Party

North Suburbs:
Bluff City Cemetery
Cuba Road
Emmerich Park
Fox River Grove School Bus Accident
Site
Mt. Thabor Cemetery
Munger Road Train Tracks
Chicago O'Hare International Airport
Sheraton Gateway Suites Hotel at
O'Hare
American Airlines Flight 191
Disaster Site
Raceway Woods
Randall Road and State Route 72
Intersection
River Valley Memorial Gardens
Robinson Woods Forest Preserve
Shoe Factory Road
Sunrise Park
The Gate

Trout Park
White Cemetery
Tyrell Road Cemetery
Antioch Downtown Theater
Channing Park and School
Dead Man's Creek
Hotel Baker
Huntley Grease Factory
Blood's Point Road
Colonel Palmer House
Algonquin Cemetery
Square Barn Road
Al Capone's Hideaway and Steakhouse
Covered Bridge Trails

South Suburbs:

Bachelor's Grove Cemetery
Burr Oak Cemetery
Cantigny
Frank "The Enforcer" Nitti's Suicide
   Site
German Church Road
Holy Sepulcher Cemetery
Mount Carmel Cemetery
Naperville Cemetery

Archer Woods Cemetery
Maple Lake
Willowbrook Ballroom
Irish Legend Pub and Restaurant
Archer Avenue
Resurrection Cemetery
St. James Sag Cemetery
Rialto Square Theatre
Arcada Theatre
Leland Tower Suites
Baymont Inn and Suites
Evangelical Church Cemetery (Oak
   Brook)
Cigars and Stripes BBQ Lounge
Country House Restaurant
Ivy
Fort Dearborn Massacre Site
Queen of Heaven Cemetery
County Farm Cemetery (Joliet Potter's
   Field)
Joliet Arsenal
Manteno State Hospital
Woodlawn Cemetery
Axeman's Bridge

APPENDIX II
DAYTRIPPING [or in this case, NIGHTTRIPPING]

THE PARANORMAL PUB CRAWL
The Best Spirits in Town!

1ST STOP: Green Mill Cocktail Lounge

2ND STOP: Fireside Lounge

3RD STOP: Edgewater Lounge

4TH STOP: Liar's Club

5TH STOP: Smart Bar

6TH STOP: Tonic Room

7TH STOP: Clark Street Ale House

(Remember, do not drive drunk. The city has enough ghosts. We don't want you making more.)

SPEND A WEEK SLEEPING AROUND
Make sure you bring protection...

SUNDAY: Stay in room 208 at the Baymont Inn and Suites

MONDAY: Congress Hotel

TUESDAY: Hotel Baker

WEDNESDAY: Leland Tower Suites

THURSDAY: Sheraton Gateway Suites Hotel at O'Hare

FRIDAY: House of Blues and Hotel Sax

SATURDAY: By this time, you'll need a stay at the Manteno State Hospital for the insane.

ARCHER AVENUE
The Most Haunted Road in America

1ST STOP: Start, as Resurrection Mary did, at the Willowbrook Ballroom

2ND STOP: Stop for a drink at Irish Legend Pub and Restaurant across the street

3RD STOP: Drive down Archer Avenue, looking for Resurrection Mary

4TH STOP: Stop at Resurrection Cemetery to visit Resurrection Mary's grave

5TH STOP: Might as well visit St. James Sag Cemetery while you're here

CHICAGO TRAGEDY TOUR
In remembrance of those places that most would sooner forget

1ST STOP: Start at the Chicago Water Tower, which survived the Great Chicago Fire

2ND STOP: Go to the Eastland Disaster Site at the Chicago River

3RD STOP: then to the site of the Ford Center for the Performing Arts Oriental Theatre fire

4TH STOP: Go to American Airlines Flight 191 Disaster Site

5TH STOP: then to the Fox River Grove School Bus Accident Site

6TH STOP: end at Queen of Heaven Cemetery to remember those lost in the Our Lady of the Angels School fire

GANGLAND
My Jesus Mercy

1ST STOP: Visit Death Corner in Little Hell, where the Black Hand dumped bodies

2ND STOP: Visit the Green Mill Cocktail Lounge, a Prohibition-era speakeasy run by the Chicago Outfit

3RD STOP: Visit the site of the St. Valentine's Day Massacre

4TH STOP: Visit the site where Al Capone's must trusted lieutenant, Frank Nitti, killed himself

5TH STOP: Visit Al Capone's grave at Mount Carmel Cemetery

6TH STOP: Visit the Biograph Theater where John Dillinger was killed

APPENDIX III

PLACES THAT DID NOT QUITE MAKE THE BOOK

HARPO STUDIOS

REASON IT DIDN'T MAKE THE BOOK: Oprah left
REASON WE WANTED IT IN THE BOOK: *It's one of the most famous haunted locations in the city.*

When 844 people died in the middle of the city in the Eastland Disaster, the bodies had to be stored somewhere. The place they chose as a temporary morgue was most recently Harpo Studios. When the studios were being used to tape Oprah Winfrey's daily talk show, tons of ghosts haunted the hallways of the studio. People reported hearing laughing from empty halls. Footsteps would also echo down these empty halls. Sounds of crying, apparitions, and a mysterious "gray lady" have also been reported throughout these studios.

Unfortunately, now that Oprah's show has ended and she has left the studios, shows are no longer taped here. Thus, it is completely off limits to the public. Tours are not even offered of the studios. Because we want to give readers a chance to see the ghosts in the chapters of this book, we had to leave this location out.

RED LION PUB

REASON IT DIDN'T MAKE THE BOOK: Closed
REASON WE WANTED IT IN THE BOOK: *A famous haunted bar across the street from the Biograph Theater*

The Red Lion Pub was one of the most famous haunted bars in the Chicagoland area. It was supposedly haunted by the spirit of the man who founded the bar after World War II. Ghost enthusiasts from all around Chicagoland would make sure to go to the Red Lion Pub, and many books about the area included stories about the bar. People heard footsteps throughout the bar. Doors opened and closed by themselves. The ghost of the former owner actually appeared in photographs taken by unsuspecting bar patrons.

When I (Jeff) first visited Chicago to meet up with Vince and visit some of the haunted locations, we decided that we would take in a Reds and Cubs game over at Wrigley Field. We arrived early and decided to stay on the train for one more stop, exiting near the Biograph Theater and Red Lion Pub, locations we planned to add to the book. We walked through the alley beside the Biograph where Dillinger died and then looked across the street expecting to see the Red Lion Pub. Instead, there was simply a boarded-up storefront where the pub once stood. We were unable to find any plans that the Red Lion would be reopening, so we had to omit it.

JOHN WAYNE GACY'S HOUSE

REASON IT DIDN'T MAKE THE BOOK: Somebody lives there
REASON WE WANTED IT IN THE BOOK: *We didn't have any John Wayne Gacy locations*

John Wayne Gacy is one of the most famous serial killers of all time. Throughout his career as a killer, he murdered at least 33 young boys. Most of the bodies of these boys were deposited into the crawlspace that ran underneath Gacy's house. When the horror of his crimes finally came to light, police began searching his house. It wasn't until they accessed the crawlspace and began finding body after body that the true horror of what had occurred came to light. Ghosts of those who died in the house supposedly still haunt the place.

The house was purchased by a private owner. Because someone actually lives in this house, it isn't accessible to members of the public looking for ghosts. Furthermore, we didn't want people going to this person's house and taking pictures from the outside or sneaking around the property, so we opted to leave it out altogether.

JACKSON PARK

ALREADY HAD WORLD'S FAIR LOCATIONS IN THE AREA
REASON WE WANTED IT IN THE BOOK: *I really like anything having to do with the World's Fair*

The grass and trails through Jackson Park cover the very land on which the 1893 Chicago World's Fair took place. People report seeing figures walking the trails at night that then vanish. People hear voices and feel the energy of the fair that took place here 120 years ago. Furthermore, the park is open until 11 p.m., making it an even better place to sit and look for ghosts.

The reason that we left this park out of the book was because we featured two other locations that abut the park and have very similar ghost stories. The Clarence Darrow Memorial Bridge is in the park itself, as is the Museum of Science and Industry. Because we already feature these locations and speak of the ghosts of the World's Fair in these and other chapters, we figured we would leave Jackson Park out of the book.

APPENDIX IV
LOCAL PARANORMAL GROUPS

Chicago Paranormal Investigators: chicagoparanormalinvestigators.org

Yours truly, Vince Sheilds, started this investigation group, which is located in the city of Chicago. Its experts have experience with negative entities as well as positive ones, and although they use unique tools and gadgets for investigations, they rely mostly on concrete evidence. The members of this team pride themselves on adapting to each and every unique situation.

Will County Ghost Hunters: theghostpage.com

A staple in the Chicagoland area for years, this team is based in Will County, just south of Chicago's Cook County. This dependable, level-headed group takes a very logical, well-rounded approach to its investigations.

Haunted Chicago: hauntedchicago.com

Based throughout the Chicagoland area, this group of true professionals really knows its stuff. Haunted Chicago has been around long enough to know what is what, and its team members are excellent at articulating the details of each investigation. They bear a level of professionalism that is unsurpassed and are highly respected by other teams.

Nexus Paranormal Investigations: nexuspi.com

This is a relatively new group that takes a "new-school" approach to its investigations. Its team members make sure to follow the guidelines that they have set for themselves. Don't let this relatively new group fool you; it knows how to run a proper investigation. Nexus Paranormal Investigations is based throughout the Chicagoland area.

Elgin Paranormal Investigators: elginparanormalinvestigators.com

Based in Elgin, a suburb of Chicago, this group of investigators conducts thorough, complete, and no-nonsense investigations. They have been active for several years and have the experience and tools to provide great results.

Legally Dead Paranormal:
legallydeadparanormal.com

Based in the city of Chicago, this very reliable group of investigators actually has an ordained minister for a leader. This fact alone gives them a unique investigational edge.

Chicago Paranormal Investigations:
pactpara.com

In most cases, one would assume that such a youthful group of investigators would have some trouble carrying out a thorough investigation. Don't make that mistake. This is a group of forward-thinkers that makes up for any lack of experience with enthusiasm and love for the paranormal field.

Cook County Paranormal Research Team:
ccprt.com

This great group of investigators is well-rounded in numerous paranormal areas and has more than a few years of experience dealing with ghostly happenings. Everyone on this team seems to play his own specific part in aiding an investigation, which leads to highly successful results. Its members are based throughout the Cook County (Chicago) area.

Paranormal Anomaly Research Team:
pastinvestigators.com

PAST was formed in 2006. This group of true professionals has conducted investigations longer than the members of most paranormal investigation groups have been alive. This team's experience, combined with a collective love for and dedication to all things weird and paranormal, ensures that they'll provide an informative and complete investigation.

ABOUT the AUTHORS

JEFF MORRIS

JEFF MORRIS WAS BORN in the late 70s in Cincinnati, Ohio, so will likely die in the 2040s or 2050s. He graduated with a degree in writing from Miami University in Oxford, Ohio in 2000 and has been interested in paranormal phenomena since 2005. In 2006, he founded a ghost tour in Miamitown, Ohio with his brother which still runs to this day. This is Jeff's fourth book. He published his first book, *Haunted Cincinnati and Southwest Ohio* in 2009 and has published 1 book per year since then with *Cincinnati Haunted Handbook* in 2010, *Nashville Haunted Handbook* in 2011, and *Twin Cities Haunted Handbook* in 2012. Jeff currently resides in Cincinnati with his wife and two children who will likely die in 2062, 2089, and 2101 respectively.

VINCE SHEILDS

VINCE SHEILDS WAS BORN in Elgin, IL in 1984. He enlisted in the Marine Corps in 2002 and, upon discharge in 2006, moved to Chicago where his fascination with the paranormal really took form. There he formed his website for Chicago Paranormal Investigators with his teammates. They started investigating local haunted hot spots, Chicago favorites, and private homes."